THE STORY ARC

Practical and Persuasive Magic for Authors,
Speakers and Product Creators

KELLAN FLUCKIGER

RED AUSSIE
— PUBLISHING —

Published in Phoenix, Arizona, by Red Aussie Publishing
22424 S Ellsworth Loop Rd
Unit 898
Queen Creek, AZ 85142
Contact the Publisher: RedAussiePublishing@gmail.com
Or www.RedAussiePublishing.com
Contact the author:
www.KellanFluckiger.com

Printed in the United States of America
First Printing 2020
First Edition 2020

ISBN: 978-1-9994945-8-2

Red Aussie Publishing CEO: Joy Fluckiger
Cover Art & Layout: Joy Fluckiger

THE STORY ARC

TABLE OF CONTENTS

FOREWORD

In my former career as a corporate speaker and trainer, I would often work with sales teams to help them "get their numbers up" as they put it, by which they meant *sell more.*

I used a version of the former work I'd done with non-profit fundraisers that helped them raise more money for their cause.

In each case, the emphasis was on telling stories rather than pitching features and benefits. Why did I do this? It made the numbers get better...and it raised more money.

But why, exactly, did it do that? Because stories enter the human system through the right brain, not the left. Stories have people picture things (right brain) instead of critiquing and analyzing things with skepticism (left brain).

And, therefore, as the author Libby Bray says, "There is no greater power on this earth than story." And as marketing genius Seth Godin says, "Marketing is no longer about the stuff that you make, but about the stories you tell."

As well as I thought I knew those truths back then (because, yes, those training sessions got good enough results for my clients) I do wish I had been able to have this book by Kellan Fluckiger at my fingertips to read and re-read. I would have been able to retire much sooner. Because *The Story Arc* reveals the underside of the weave, the secret of the clearest *how to* when it comes to story-telling!

Before I tell you about this amazing book you are now about to read (and re-read), one more quote feels appropriate, from the brilliant social analyst and author Daniel Pink, "The future belongs to a different kind of person with a different kind of mind: artists, inventors, storytellers---creative and holistic 'right-brain' thinkers."

This book shows you the way to become creative and holistic in your work. Take it in deeply, and the future belongs to you as well. Because that "different kind of mind that Daniel Pink talks about is not inherent...it can be learned, and this book has that precise teaching.

Most "how to" books are written by people who are better at presenting theories about how to do things than they are at actually doing them. Whenever I see books about "how to make a fortune in the stock market" I wonder why the author doesn't just go make a fortune in the stock market instead of trying to eke out a living selling his little book?

If he really knew how to, I'm sure he would have done it himself. This phenomenon of theory-only practitioners has led to the cynical bromide, "Those who can, do..... those who can't, teach."

Fortunately for readers of this book, Kellan has had a long history of masterful story-telling behind him prior to writing this book. He's written 11 books, all of them spellbinding with stories drawn from his own life. I've also personally seen him in recent years telling stories in front of a room full of people who were not only mesmerized, but also moved to new creative action because of his talks.

Even in this book, Kellan tells captivating stories. They serve his mission of giving you an amazingly practical system he calls The Story Arc. It's what he himself has learned to use. And the result? He says it right here:

"Suddenly organizing and then writing books became easy. By being clear with myself about what I thought the reader might or might not already know, I was able to include instructions about chapters they could skip or others they could emphasize depending on their existing knowledge."

"That gave me confidence the reader would be able to follow the story and teaching no matter what their skill level or previous experience."

"It was like magic and it made every book from then on fun to organize and a joy to write. I was no longer worried about anything in the process."

What if your own creative project became easy? What if you had a system (filled with insights about the creative process) that made your own project fun to organize and a joy to write? This book is a practical field manual for exactly that.

Kellan Fluckiger is one of those rare powerful life and business coaches whose books actually coach people as powerfully as he himself does. In this book, he shows *you* (and me) how to do that too. You'll enjoy the journey through the three stages of the book, learning all the way to 1) Tell your story, 2) Teach your truth, and

3) Change the world. (The very things Kellan himself has done with his previous books, and now, especially, with this one.)

What better use of one's life would there be but to do as this book teaches: Tell your story, teach your truth and change the world?

Steve Chandler

Birmingham, Michigan

June, 2020

INTRODUCTION

There are thousands of books on storytelling, how to write books, and how to make a difference in the world. Why would I write another book about the same topic?

We live in a time of rapid change. Everyone can put their opinion in the marketplace. Everyone can share their method for getting something done. This can be a good thing, and it can also be very confusing.

I'm writing this book for three reasons:

1. I have written 11 books. This is my 12th, and I have several more on the drawing board. In the process of writing and publishing, I found tools and shortcuts that help me:

- Get clear about the message I want to share.

- Connect well with my audience.

- Move people to action.

I want to share these tools.

2. As a coach, I regularly hear a confusing contradiction. People often tell me they want to "help others" in various ways. Usually this includes writing a book. When we start talking about a book, I then hear: "I have nothing special to say." Upon further questioning, it becomes clear the person I'm talking to has extraordinary experience and perspective that will be very beneficial to a particular audience.

The feeling of "having nothing to say," or "not being important" is commonplace and misplaced.

What any individual has to say may or may not be important to millions. It doesn't need to be important to millions to be valuable to those who read it. This book will provide encouragement and direction to those who believe they have something to say and feel either afraid or unsure about how to do it.

3. Because publishing and spreading ideas is easier than ever, it's important to be able to be clear, concise, and powerful in your messaging if you want to be heard at all. The sheer volume of published content is so large that it's hard to be heard above the noise. Whether you write a book, create a program, or speak from stage, clarity, and relevance are essential. I want to help make that happen for those with a message.

I am not claiming what I present here is the only way or the best way to write books, create programs, design workshops, or keynote speeches. It's a set of helpful and repeatable processes I use with my work and with many clients.

As you experiment with the ideas here, you will undoubtedly modify them to suit your own message and work style. I expect that to happen. The fundamental principles will still serve you as a framework to build your own production machinery.

This book is for people who want to write nonfiction. It is geared toward those who use their own growth stories as a basis for personal improvement and help or advice they give to others. It is also for those writing books based on their own learning and experience in any field outside personal development.

Besides writing books, this work is for those who create content of any kind. The Story Arc™ has been used to create multi-day workshops, online courses, and products and keynote speeches. Any communication where the audience goes on a journey designed to change their thinking, learn new paradigms, or get rid of old habits is a perfect application of the Story Arc™.

This book is not designed as a writing course. Elements of style and grammar are not addressed. It's not a course for fictional character development or plot coherence. Those looking to write the next *Lord of the Rings* trilogy will need to seek help elsewhere.

If you want to write a story about things that happened to you, then describe how you grew from these events and present it to help others with similar or related problems, this is exactly what you need.

The book has three sections. They will reflect the three parts of the Story Arc™ journey. Part One is, "Tell Your Story." This part will teach you how to create a "developmental story" that tracks your own learning and development as you went through life and had the experiences that gave you your current point of view and wisdom.

Part Two is "Teach Your Truth." This part will show you how to organize what you learned from your life experience, so it's easy to teach others and help them internalize it for their benefit.

Part Three is "Change the World." No enlightenment or discovery, however fantastic, will have any impact at all until it is shared. Today there are thousands of ways to "put your stuff out there." This part will give you ideas and direction to leverage what you have written to maximize your audience, grow your impact, and make money from your work.

Everything I tell you in this book has been battle-tested and proven to be effective. I know from my own experience things that work and some that don't. I will share everything I know with you and expect that you will adapt it for your best use.

Having said all that, I write this with the greatest of love for those who have a message to share and have drummed up the courage to insert their message in the marketplace.

PROLOGUE

I sat in the audience riveted by the speaker on stage. I followed every nuance of the story and identified with the emotions he described.

He told his own story starting from when he was nine years old. He described hopes and dreams and travails and setbacks. He poured out his heart and had us all feeling the determination that had accompanied different events along the way.

It was compelling, funny, and educational all at the same time. It was easy to see how he had such accolades as an amazing speaker and a magnificent teacher of the art of storytelling.

As the applause died down, I was feeling emotional. Tears were running down my cheeks, and I buried my head in my hands.

At first, I wasn't even sure what I was feeling. I thought it was an emotional reaction to his triumphant story and all the twists and turns that brought the tears.

After a few minutes, I realized I was feeling frustration, helplessness, and perhaps a tinge of jealousy. Maybe there was some anger sneaking around the edge somewhere.

"Of course," I exclaimed in my mind, "I could speak on stage powerfully if I had a story like that to tell." "I mean, come on, anyone with a story that amazing and powerful could captivate an audience and keep them riveted for an hour or two."

"Me, I got nothing."

I convinced myself that there was nothing in my life that was noteworthy, story-worthy, and certainly, nothing even remotely to compare with what that speaker had just given us.

I went away from the conference feeling hard done by, duped and frustrated. I did not purchase the upsell tickets to the extra event that was offered. That second event was to learn to develop your own story and tell it in such a way as to gather an audience and create a tribe.

But those are exactly the things I wanted to do. I was a brand-new coach, and I felt like I was a good one. I enjoyed great success as a consultant and was well known for my ability to help individuals and teams accomplish difficult things.

Somehow in my mind that previous success translated into being a good coach. I supposed those skills would be useful in coaching, but I needed, or at least I thought I did, to create a compelling narrative and gather a tribe.

I had been excited about coming to this conference because of the promised content. After listening to the story of the featured speaker, I was frustrated and disappointed not because it wasn't a great story and not because he wasn't a great speaker.

I was frustrated because I was convinced that there was nothing in my life that would allow me to create and tell a compelling story so I could teach the truth I had and make a difference in the world like the speaker was doing.

Over and over again, I went to the events in my life and tried in vain to figure out how I could create some narrative or compelling story that would connect to me with an audience. I knew or at least I thought I knew that without the audience, I would not be able to spread the message that I had.

The days and weeks went by, and my frustration only increased. Ten, twenty, even thirty versions of my life filled pages and pages as I vainly tried to make something I believed was good. Miserable and floundering, I felt like a failure.

I bought many courses and studied other coaches and speakers who had similar abilities. Each seemed to have a compelling narrative that set the stage to connect with them. It was working because I wanted to learn what they had to say.

Was it at all trickery? Was there a set of slick techniques I needed to learn to "cast the spell" over the audience and make them listen to me with rapt attention?

As a consultant, I had spoken as a keynote speaker at conferences around the world. But that was about a technical subject on which I was a world-class expert and where I had no trouble organizing my thoughts and presenting conclusions and predictions with strong backing.

When it came to my own life and story, I felt just the same as I did when I left the conference months earlier. "Me, I got nothing."

PART I

TELL YOUR STORY

Why tell a story in the first place? Why can't I just launch into teaching the audience what I know to be true from my own experience?

As it turns out, how much I teach doesn't matter. It also doesn't matter how well I teach. The only thing that matters is how much the audience hears, takes in deeply, and remembers long enough to put into action.

Humans are a storytelling species. For thousands of years, truth, societal norms, sacred practices, family traditions, and values of all kinds have been shared through storytelling.

Even skills for survival, growing food, and making tools and equipment have been peppered with stories about how to do it right and what happens when we do it wrong.

There are three main reasons that stories work.

1. Stories are memorable.

2. Stories are powerful.

3. Stories are long-lasting.

When my children were young, especially when they were under ten years old, I found that I could keep all of them busy and entertained if I told a story. I was never very good at remembering old folktales or fairy tales. So, I made up my own stories.

I had no idea how powerful they would be and how deeply they would sink until year after year, as we went on some outing or campground, the kids would ask me to tell a story I had told before. That happened over and over again. It was funny because I couldn't remember the stories myself.

I made them up as I went along, and so I didn't remember all the parts. That turned out okay because they remembered the story far better than I did. They helpfully filled in details as we re-created the stories together.

This example taught me a valuable lesson about how memorable stories can be.

Every one of us has experienced hearing a story that has moved us emotionally. I remember a story my uncle told me when I was a child.

It was a story about two steeplejacks. A steeplejack is a person who works on high structures like church steeples, clock towers, and other tall buildings. Typically, such work is for maintenance, painting, or other repairs.

In this story, two brothers were working on a church steeple. The repair they were doing required the use of molten lead. As you know, molten lead is about 600°F.

The story was from the 1800s, and the craftsmen were not using safety harnesses like we might see today. One brother was standing on the other's shoulders on top of the scaffolding.

The topmost brother spilled some of the molten lead on his brother below. The lead burned into his arm, causing enormous pain. Any normal person would have recoiled because of the burn.

The brother on the bottom, determined to be strong and not endanger his sibling, withstood the pain until the brother above climbed down to safety. If he had cringed and recoiled, the sibling perched on his shoulders surely would have plunged to his death.

I cried when I heard it then, and I still get emotional when I think about it now. The lesson for me then, and forever, was one of determination and courage. I wanted to be that courageous brother.

Indigenous people are legendary for using storytelling to pass tradition and spiritual and religious values from generation to generation. This has been the practice for thousands of years. Today we use many "ancient legends" to illustrate values and to teach principles.

These stories and legends have stood the test of time and have been repeated millions of times over thousands of years. There is no question that stories are eternal.

Since we know these things about stories, mastering the art of storytelling in conjunction with teaching important lessons about life is powerful and useful.

Most self-help books derived from personal experience are designed to help the reader avoid pitfalls, learn difficult lessons, and make progress faster than the person telling the story.

This only happens when it is done well. This first part of the book is about how to create your personal story and how to use it to create the kind of connection necessary, so your audience hears you and feels you are real.

Chapter 1

The Cab Ride Part I

Candace came out of the train station and squinted at the sun. It was late afternoon, and warmer than she expected, and the glare made it hard to see. She was fashionably dressed in a bright red dress and carried a small black designer clutch.

She followed the signs toward the Taxi stand and looked around for one marked "Opera Express." She saw it immediately. There was no one in line. At least she didn't have to wait too long in the sun.

The directions on her smartphone said it was about a ½ hour cab ride from the train station to the opera house. She always checked the route because she heard stories about crooked cabbies who ran up the meter by taking the long way. She was looking forward to some quiet time with nothing to do.

She was not happy about having to spend the night going to the opera. She never understood what any of the singers were singing about, and the lavish costumes looked silly and pointless.

She was going to miss her favorite TV shows and a night at home, but her boss had been clear about the need to accept the opera tickets and make nice with the client who had given them to her firm.

Frustrated about the assignment and a little grumpy about the weather, she slid into the back seat of the cab, slouched down in the seat, and already wished that the half-hour drive was over.

She hoped the cabbie would keep quiet because she was in no mood for idle chitchat on the way to a place she didn't want to go, in a city she didn't want to be in and wasting time she didn't have to waste.

"Good afternoon, ma'am." Came the cheery voice from the front seat. She groaned inwardly and mumbled a response.

"Going to the opera, are we?"

"This is the Opera Express, right? She answered, slightly sarcastically.

"Just checking, you'd be surprised how often people don't read the words on the door."

"Yes, I'm going, but not of my choice."

"Well, I'm sure you'll enjoy the show. Have you been to the opera much?"

"A time or two. I'm really not much of a fan. it's always boring, and I can't understand what's going on anyway."

"You know, I used to feel exactly the same way about the opera."

Surprised, she said, "Are you a big opera fan?" Somehow, she didn't expect the cab driver to know anything about the opera, let alone be an aficionado.

"Yes," came the enthusiastic reply. "I think knowing something about the opera was one of the reasons I got the job. The opera house is quite picky about who drives their patrons to the show."

Once again, she was a bit surprised. Somehow the cheery temperament and the surprise revelation that this man knew something about the opera got her attention, just a little.

"How do you even tell what's going on in the story?" She queried.

"Some operas are a lot harder to follow than others. The one you're going to see tonight is actually one of the easier ones to connect with."

"Yeah, I guess we'll see." She looked at her phone, hoping that the driver would notice her intentional shift in focus and stop trying to make her enjoy something she was certain would be a disaster.

After just a minute of silence, the driver spoke once again. "Sorry I didn't introduce myself, I'm Bill, and I've been driving this cab to the opera for ten years. I love it."

Surprised again, she wondered how someone could enjoy driving a cab at all, let alone for ten years. She wanted to end the conversation but somehow felt like she had to ask one more question.

"Okay, I'll bite. Why do you get such a kick out of driving people to the opera?"

"Well, you meet all kinds of people. Some folks know a lot about the shows they're going to see. I love listening to them talk about the music or the story on the way. That's one of the ways I learned as much as I have about each opera. You'd be surprised at the different opinions people have."

She looked out the window at the surroundings and realized they were stopped at a complicated six-point intersection. "This light sure is taking forever," She complained.

"There's no way to avoid this intersection on the way from the train station to the opera house. Nobody likes it, and it has earned its own name, The Death Star. Not because there are a lot of accidents, but because you get bored to death while waiting. The star comes from the six points in the intersection."

The light changed, and they started moving. "Finally," she muttered under her breath.

Undeterred by her pessimistic mood, Bill continues. "You asked earlier how to understand the storyline and follow what's going on. I can give you some tips if you like to make the show more fun tonight."

Realizing that it was hopeless to wish the cabbie would be silent, she decided to play along. "Okay, tell me. At least that way, it might be a little less boring."

"The first thing to do is to know a little bit about the story before you go. Sometimes they give you a brochure with the story, but it's usually better to take just five minutes and look the opera up online. That way, you know the character names, the storyline, so it makes sense."

"Okay, that makes sense."

"Since I'm sure you didn't have time to do that, let me tell you just a little bit about why this opera tonight is so much fun. First of all, it's a story of mystery and intrigue. There's love involved, jealousy, excitement, and triumph in the end.

"Really, all that is in the story?"

"Yes, it is, and I'll tell you how to prepare yourself so you can follow it."

She decided this wasn't as bad as she thought and leaned forward a bit in the seat so she could pay more attention and not miss any of the good stuff.

CHAPTER 2

THE CAB RIDE PART II

He considered for a moment the best way to help Candace understand the upcoming show. She waited expectantly while he was lost for a moment in thought. Then with a smile, he began.

"I mentioned before, I used to think the opera was boring and didn't enjoy it all. I was driving a cab for another company and happened to have a passenger who was going to the opera."

"I ask him if he really enjoyed the spectacle. He told me that it was wonderful, and he loved every minute of it. I told him that to me, it was unintelligible nonsense."

"That's about where I am," quipped Candace.

"We had about 45 minutes in the car, and during that time, he told me the whole story of the opera he was going to see. I listened politely at first and then realized the story was fascinating. I began to ask a bunch of questions, and because of his deep knowledge, he was able to answer them well.

"So that changed your mind?"

"No, not all at once, but it sent me on a path of thinking. I realized I had been judging something without knowing anything about it. I decided to learn just a little more."

"What did you do?"

"I bought tickets to that very same opera a week later. I decided to see for myself what the experience was. He had given me some advice about how to prepare, and I followed it."

"What did he tell you?"

He paused for a moment and thought. Candace looked around and realized they were just passing a large building with the sign on the front "Public Library."

"There were three parts to the advice. It works for me, and I'll share it with you, and maybe you'll get some benefit from it."

"Is it complicated?"

Not really. It doesn't take much time either because most of the preparation is not about doing something; it's about the way you think about the situation and how you approach the event."

"What do you mean?"

"The first step is the only one that takes any time at all." It's a simple choice, really. You just spend 20 minutes or so reading about the opera, the story, and the people that are playing the lead roles."

"What does that do?"

"I found it drew me into the story. I learned a little bit about when it was composed, the story the composer was trying to tell, and some interesting things about the people on stage. It made them just a little bit more like real people instead of just somebody up there on stage doing something."

"Okay, I hadn't thought about it like that. I never even thought about the people behind the mask of the singing and acting on stage."

"I used to do that too. After I spent the time to learn just a little bit about it, suddenly I had an interest. I started wondering how this particular actor was going to portray their role in the story and how it all would feel."

"That doesn't seem like a big deal. After you spend some time getting familiar with the characters, the story, and the actors and actresses in the lead roles, what's next?"

"You're right, it isn't hard, but you do need to dedicate the 20 minutes to make it happen."

For a moment, Candace considered the thought of preparation. She reflected on how many things she did without adequate preparation and the consequences of that kind of approach to things.

"I guess that's probably true for everything, isn't it?" She wasn't sure if he had heard her comment because it was quiet and mostly to herself. Then he spoke again.

"Part two of the preparation takes no time at all because it is all in your head. On the way to the show, I review the story in my mind, and I make a simple choice. I choose to go to this show with nothing else on my mind, but following the story, watching the people on stage portray the parts and getting caught up in the music."

"Isn't that hard?"

"It's just a choice. You're going to spend time getting to the show anyway. You get to decide what you do in your mind with that time. If you're busy doing other things, then your out of sync with the event when you get there."

She considered the implications of what Bill said. "Kind of like having an argument on the way to a meeting. You get there, and you're all flustered and completely unprepared. Then you either need to take a break before you start or spend the first 15 minutes getting your bearings."

"Exactly."

"I think I get it. If I spend the time traveling to the event completely focused on what's coming up, then I'll be in the mood and ready to go when I get there." She thought again about where else this approach might be useful. "So, then what?"

"Part three doesn't take any time either. It's another choice and then some activity in your mind."

"So, it's mostly just a head game?" She laughed a bit and thought about the head games people played in her office.

"You're going to spend over two hours in your seat in the opera house. People performing up on the stage will be giving everything they've got. If you have done step one and step two, you're in the mood and ready to be entertained."

She sat lost in thought for a moment and noticed that they were passing a busy gas station with a long line of cars. "I can see that, so what is step three?"

"It is a choice that during the performance, you are fully present to what is happening. You go all in. You think about nothing at all except the story you are familiar with, the nuances of the performance and the beauty of what is happening in front of you."

"I think I'm starting to get this."

"If you turn off your cell phone, all the way off and not even on vibrate and pay 100% attention to the people on stage, magic happens. Ignore the people sitting next to you, ignore the coughs and the paper rustling, and completely focus on the event you came to see.

You're going to be sitting there either way. You took the time to prepare. You might as well go all in and be completely focused.

"You're right. I'm going to be sitting there for that time anyway. If I'm busy thinking about other things or the people around me, I will miss important elements, and I won't have any idea what's happening."

"I can promise you if you choose to follow these three steps, your experience at the opera will be completely different. I certainly know mine was. Before I learned this, I didn't consider myself a fan at all. I learned everything from my passenger that day."

Candace reflected on the three steps she just heard. Not difficult, but so easily overlooked. She marveled at how the same three things could affect so many areas in her personal and professional life.

They turned a corner, and Candace saw in the distance the flag that flew over the opera house. She also saw a four-story building on the right with lots of windows and the sign "City Hall."

CHAPTER 3

THE CAB RIDE PART III

C andace realized that the drive would be over in a few minutes. The time had passed quickly, and her mood had changed completely.

She was now leaning forward even more and earnestly engaged in this back-and-forth with Bill, her cab driver. She also realized that she had judged the whole situation poorly.

She wondered where else in her life this kind of judgment and lack of attention was showing up. She made a silent promise to herself to think more about that later. Right now, she wanted badly to finish this conversation.

As she thought more deeply, she said, almost to herself, "You know, this preparation approach might make a difference in a lot of things. I wonder if it's as powerful as it seems?"

Quietly he said, "I don't know for sure how it will work out for you, but you can try it today and see what happens."

"I'd love to tell you about the results afterward." She said, almost to herself.

"About a month ago, I had another passenger who felt kind of the same about the whole opera experience. I gave him pretty much the same set of instructions, and he was so excited that he asked me to come back and pick him up afterward. I don't usually do that, but he was so determined that I decided to. It worked like magic."

"I'd really be interested in telling you what happens to me." Are you still on duty when the performance finishes?"

"Yes." He said. "Do you have an appointment after the show?"

"The client I'm meeting with had talked about going somewhere for a bite after the event."

"I'd be happy to come and pick up both of you out and take you to your restaurant."

"That would be marvelous. I think it will be fun to tell you what happened, even with someone else along for the ride."

"Okay, I'll be back in about 3 ½ hours." He said, looking at his watch.

They pulled up to the building, and the cab came to a stop. She looked at the time and realized there were still a few minutes before she was supposed to meet her client. "I think I've only done one of the three things you told me."

"What do you mean?"

"Well, I am completely prepared to go into the performance and be all in as you instructed." But I didn't do any research and don't know anything about the show I'm about to see."

He paused for a moment and then said, "You're right. I didn't tell you about the show yet. I can take a few minutes now and give you some detail about both the story and the actors."

"Would you be willing to do that?" The surprise was evident in her voice. Candace expected that the meter would keep running, and she would pay extra, but that was no problem because she really wanted to hear more.

"Sure," he replied happily.

His tone softened as he started. "This opera is set about 200 years ago and tells the story of an ill-fated romance between a nobleman's daughter and the son of a commoner..."

He went on for about 10 minutes and gave her a good summary of the story, emphasizing the dramatic parts but not giving away all the plot twists and certainly not the ending.

When he finished, she realized her eyes had been closed from concentration. She looked outside and saw another car pulling up and the client she was supposed to meet stepping out.

"There's the man I'm supposed to meet for the opera. Thank you so much for taking the time to tell me the story. I feel fully ready and excited to go in and immerse myself in this experience. I'll bet my client doesn't know anywhere near as much about this story as I do. Maybe I'll be able to help him enjoy the experience also."

"Maybe you will, and won't that be exciting? It might even help with your business, who knows?"

"Thank you again; I never imagined looking forward to an opera. This has made a tremendous difference for me. I think it will matter in other areas in my life as I look to see what these three steps might do elsewhere."

"You're more than welcome, and I'll see you after the show."

"Yes, you will, and I can't wait to tell you how it all goes. How much do I owe you?"

He motioned toward the meter and repeated the numbers on the screen. She noticed that the numbers had not changed since they stopped. He had not charged her for the waiting time as he told the story.

She reflected on the service that he gave to help her have a good time and a successful business event. She said nothing about the meter but tipped him generously.

"Thank you," he said.

"Thank you ever so much more, and I'll see you in a few hours."

She exited the cab and walked toward her business contact. Bill watched the enthusiasm she displayed as she greeted her client. He knew it would be a good meeting.

Chapter 4

What Happened?

In the last three chapters, I told a fictional story about an imaginary cab ride from a train station to an opera house. Nothing was particularly remarkable. There were no accidents and no unusual events.

This simple story at the start is to help you understand that writing a book or creating a course to help others to change something is not difficult, follows a straightforward process, and does not require remarkable events.

The cab ride is the analogy I use when explaining The Story Arc™ process. It is something everyone understands easily and is also the container for a powerful message. It illustrates the key steps required to take someone on an emotional journey.

The three key steps are:

1. Connect with someone authentically.

2. Teach them something they need.

3. Show them it will work *for them*.

Let's look at the key players of the trip.

First, there is the passenger, Candace. A typical businesswoman with an assignment she doesn't particularly want to do believes it will be boring and likely a waste of time.

She is stuck in the belief that the opera is for other people, and she has no interest in this art form. Whatever her previous experience, that attitude alone can spoil the evening and create poison in the business relationship.

Of course, that would be unintentional and the furthest thing from her desires. Likely, she would intend to put on a pleasant attitude and enjoy the evening.

Alternatively, she might ruefully describe her inexperience and beg for the tolerance of her fellow participant in the event. Both these alternatives are second best.

Second, there is the cab driver, Bill. He is excited about his work and notices her air of dissatisfaction. Unbeknownst to her, he has decided to help Candace with the situation. He has an experience in his life that seems appropriate to the situation. He is also willing to share with her in hopes of creating some benefit.

Third, there is the journey itself. Moving from one place to another. The physical journey from the train station to the opera house represents the emotional journey that any person might take by reading a book, taking a course, or having any interaction for learning.

Fourth, are the landmarks along the way. In any journey, some landmarks mark your progress. Following these landmarks keeps you on track and lets you know how far you've come and what's left to get to the destination.

The story serves as a model of the process for taking your own client on a journey designed to help them with a problem. The purpose of this book is to help you understand how to create this journey and teach something you believe will help others.

Whether you write a book, create a course, teach a seminar, organize a workshop or give a keynote speech, you are in the process of helping someone go on an emotional journey from point A to point B.

As I have written many books over the years and helped others do the same, it has become clear to me that a system to help organize this journey would be valuable. It will demystify the book writing process and remove the fear from teaching what you know.

Candace starts with an attitude of resignation and has no interest in anything but getting through the night. That might be just like a person who comes to a speech you might give or a seminar you might teach.

They may not want to be there and may not believe you have anything to help them. They may simply be waiting for it all to be over.

The action took place in three separate stages, following the three keys I listed above. First, Bill created a connection by helping Candace understand he didn't like opera to start with.

She was able to see that someone just like her had changed their opinion. They had gone from not understanding and not liking something to looking forward to it and being eager to participate.

In the second part of the trip, the cab driver gave her information and teaching. His gift was the three steps to have fun going to the opera.

Because she had a connection that came by knowing he previously disliked the opera, she was more open to the possibility that the three steps he gave her would work.

If he simply told her what to do to start with, it would've bounced right off and not gone into her consciousness. The act of creating rapport and some openness was the first key. Then the teaching sank in and became valuable.

The third part was getting her excited about the application of the three steps. The fact she was now prepared to go into the opera instead of being apathetic changed the game. The additional benefit of being able to help her client got her even more excited.

The invitation to continue the dialogue after the performance also added to the connection and the effectiveness of the teaching.

Our cab ride is a brief illustration of how this process works. You will see all the pieces unfold more fully as you move through the book and, at the same time, think of ways to use this process to write a book or create something else to teach what you know from your own life experience.

CHAPTER 5

DO YOU HAVE A STORY?

In the next six chapters (five through ten), we will talk about you and the questions you will have about writing a book. These are all typical concerns that authors have, especially if this is their first book or the first time they have considered writing about their own story.

The first question is the title of this chapter. Do I have a story? It's normal to wonder if you have something useful to say. The short answer is "yes." Every person in the world has unique life experiences. Even children growing up in the same household tell a completely different story about the environment at home.

My own upbringing is a perfect example. In my book *Tightrope of Depression*, I described my experience growing up. It was one of extreme physical punishment and constantly feeling not good enough.

My siblings that grew up years later in the same household don't even recognize the story I told. By then, my parents had both matured and adopted a completely different parenting style.

Same parents, same house, and same neighborhood. Completely different experience. Besides my parents changing, societal norms and other external circumstances changed. My youngest brothers and sisters might as well have grown up on another planet.

Back to the question at hand. Do you have a story?

I read a study that reported 85% of adults in the U.S. think they should write a book. That means they believe something about their life experiences is worth telling and would be of value to others.

The same study reported that less than 1% of those who think they should write a book follow through and write the book. Perhaps that is a good thing, perhaps not.

Perhaps a better version of our initial question is: "Does the story you want to tell have the potential to help those who read it?

As a coach, nearly everyone I talk to tells me, "I want to help people." Something in our nature makes us want to serve each other in profound ways.

Teenagers and college students all have a vision of doing something to change the world for the better. Few go on and do something even close to what they imagined, but the desire is universal and powerful.

There's no question you could tell a story about the experiences of your life. If you do, what's your reason for such a project? Why do you want to do this?

Would you write to make yourself feel better? Would you do it to blame others and rage out loud? Would you do it as a therapy to move forward? Is it something deeper?

Regardless of the combination of reasons you might have, the fundamental truth is that we write books, give speeches, create courses, and say what we have to say to make a difference in the world.

If you believe some people would be attracted to and benefit from what you have to say, then yes, you have a story to tell.

The 1% statistic demonstrates that few will undergo the rigors of organizing their thoughts, writing a book, and getting their message out to the world. If you are reading this, then you are among those who are considering this path.

In the prologue, I was convinced that I had nothing to share. I was certain that I had no story and certainly no "truth" that would help anyone. I knew to the core of my being that I had nothing.

Today, when I tell the story to clients and others who read my books, they stare at me incredulously. They consider my stories incredible and teachings to be valuable and powerful.

What happened?

It turns out I was wrong. I had no way to judge whether I had something useful to say. We all get used to the idea of who we are and what we have experienced. We have no way to think about it objectively to see it from the outside.

One reason for this book is to help you think critically about what you might teach and then help you organize it to serve your audience.

f you feel like I did, that you have nothing to share, then you're in the right place. The next chapters will be about helping you get your story organized and told.

Chapter 6

Life Happens

The second question is some version of "OK, stuff happened to me, and I made it. Am I ready to share?" Everywhere you look today, someone is telling their life story. Memoirs, tattletale books, and exposés of all kinds fill-up the newsstands and show up on talk shows.

Writing a book may be great therapeutic work to help you get past something. Writing about my depression certainly helped me. But that therapy was only one small motivation for the project.

I was clear from the beginning that I wanted to do something besides deal with the past and feel better.

The more I talk to prospects, clients, and people everywhere, the more I realize that everyone's life is difficult. Every single person has traumatic and complicated experiences that shape their worldview and affect their ability to perform.

Life isn't easy for anyone.

What does that mean?

If you were able to chat with someone deeply and they were vulnerable and truthful, there is not one person that doesn't have a difficult trauma of one size or another going on right now.

You lose your job and have minimal savings. An important relationship you thought was solid is suddenly in doubt or worse yet, ended. The revenue service of some state, province, or country is knocking on your door.

You get robbed. You have a massive health challenge. One of your kids gets kicked out of school for fighting, which may be the tip of the iceberg. You find yourself frustrated, depressed, and thinking that you have completely screwed up your life.

There are two main ways we cope with tough things. The first way is "day-to-day." We go gently and fearfully through the day and hope that we can "get through" what's happening now. We plead with whatever powers that be for tomorrow to be better.

Sometimes that's all we can do for a time. When you are in the thick of it, and rough things are happening all around you, it is difficult to step outside your immediate mayhem.

The second way is to slow down and be more thoughtful or philosophical about what is going on. Maybe everything happens for a reason. Maybe there is a blessing in adversity or a string of hardships.

Obviously, we don't cope just one way or the other. We operate on a sliding scale between the 'minute by minute' and the more philosophical. Our emotional capability and choices dictate where we are at any given time.

But, overall, we tend to lean towards one approach or another. Toward the coping end of the continuum, we blame others, God, and government or whatever is handy. Toward the philosophical end, we try to make sense of it all and get some balance.

You know people of both types. You may have been at both ends of the spectrum at different times in your life. I sure have. The critical piece here is to understand the choices we have and make them intentionally.

When we live at the "barely coping" end of the spectrum, we are not in a position to help anyone else much, and if we wrote a book from that place, it would be a screaming indictment of everyone and everything that has wronged us.

Those screaming books are out there, and they may be entertaining to read, but they don't do much in the way of helping the reader have a better life.

Usually, some significant event helps us move to the philosophical and balanced end of the spectrum. Sometimes this happens with age, but usually, there are precipitating events.

Events such as a life-threatening situation, a death, a massive financial reversal. Something brings us face to face with our own mortality or the ineffectiveness of how we have done things in the past.

Whatever it is, such an event or series of events causes us to reflect. We choose to take a different view of life and start asking ourselves questions.

"Do I want to keep living like I am, or do I want to change?" Or, "Is the pain of the problem worse than the struggle of the solution?" From that place, we can intentionally make changes that are good and move toward balance our lives.

When that happens, you can write to help others.

This book is to help you tell the story of your change and development *after* you have decided to become someone different – after you choose to take control of your life.

After you realize this, you might be able to help someone else who is facing similar problems to avoid some of the heartaches you've had.

When that time comes, you are ready to think about the book you might write, and the lessons you might share to help those around you.

If you are in the middle of slamming back and forth in the turmoil life offers you and still in the "screaming at life" mode, you might want to wait.

I have other books about how to get to a place of decision and power – but this isn't the book to teach that process. You can find help with that in the references in the appendix.

CHAPTER 7

GROWTH AND LEARNING

The third question is some version of "Now that I know I have a story, and I'm ready to share, will my growth and learning be useful to someone?"

If you feel the pull to write a book or create a course, it means your life has been "interesting," at least. Likely you believe it had more challenges and twists than most. If you stop to think about it, it also means you could help someone who has similar issues and challenges, if they will listen.

If you reflect on life and realize you could've saved yourself a lot of trouble and anguish if you'd paid attention to things you heard or intuitions you felt, you might feel the desire to share your experiences for the benefit of another.

Growth is a natural part of life. Wisdom is something we get gradually. There are plenty of funny sayings about "knowing everything" as a teenager and getting "dumber" as we get older. The truth is that we realize how much we didn't know and how much there is to know.

There's no question the more we live, the more we realize everything is more complicated than it seems. We realize listening, and learning is not a sign of weakness but a sign of intelligence.

This learning can help us be happier and more successful as life goes on. We make fewer mistakes, have fewer arguments, and fewer problems. If we're paying attention, we finally realize we completely create the life we have.

Learning you control what you experience and what you will create for your future is an important first step. The second step is deciding your experiences have left you with something good to share.

The third step is choosing to have the energy to organize your learning in a fashion that can be presented and absorbed by others who will benefit.

Let's use a simple example. You spend years learning how to cultivate an amazing garden. Exactly when to plant and what to plant, how to fertilize, and when and how to water. You learn the signs of the weather to protect your plants from freezing. All in all, you have become a master gardener.

Keeping accumulated wisdom for your own benefit is one choice. Most do just that. It takes a special kind of person to choose to share what they have learned.

One big challenge is your attitude about yourself. We all share a fear of inadequacy and the yearning to matter. If, like many I talk to, you believe your life has been mundane, and you don't want to embarrass yourself, then you don't understand the growth you have experienced.

You might be afraid like I was, you have nothing important to say, that no one will believe you, or worse, that no one will read your book.

Such fear is completely normal.

Though normal, the fear is not true. The great thing about your life is this: no matter where you are today, the path that got you there is unique and different. If you choose to share it and do the work to make it available, you could be a hero to someone.

Consider the societal structures we used to have: close family ties, grandparents, aunts, and uncles in the neighborhood, readily accessible relatives, and all the rest. Because the world is changing so much, those situations rarely exist, if at all.

We have become scattered and disconnected. More and more, the growth and development you have experienced is left for you alone. It helps you in your life; then, it dies with you.

Taking the opportunity to organize your thoughts and write a book might be a lifesaver for someone you don't even know. I have repeatedly had the experience of someone telling me that what I wrote changed their life forever. I would never have believed it.

On top of that, it's easier today than it has ever been to organize, publish, and use your life experience for the benefit of those around you.

CHAPTER 8

DESIRE TO SERVE

The fourth question is both a question and a choice. When you realize in your heart of hearts that you could help others with your experiences, are you willing to choose to share? People need what you have. Are you willing to walk the road of serving others?

Some people write books for a living. They create fantasy worlds and amazing fictional plots to excite and entertain. Others specialize in academic writing with significant research and footnotes on every page. Others write about history to make sure we never forget what has gone on before.

The writing and then serving I'm talking about is you choosing to share your story and teaching your readers what you have learned.

The exciting thing about our opportunity today is that the Internet and online services make it possible for someone who has never had a career as a writer to find a way to write and be useful in a meaningful way.

A common denominator among all the people I have helped write books is a desire to serve. The feeling that you could make a difference in the world if you could just communicate what you now know.

Not that many years ago, it was very difficult to make that happen. Writing a book meant laboring over a manual or electric typewriter, finishing a manuscript, finding a literary agent, writing a book proposal, and often repeating the process until you had success.

Today the desire to serve trumps everything. You can easily get the help you need to craft the story you want to tell, even if this is all new for you. I created the Story Arc™ specifically to help those who have a desire to serve by organizing and presenting their hard-won knowledge.

I had one client who has an amazing life story. I tried for years to get him to write a book. He had already written 20 books, but none of them were about his own life. While the others he wrote were good and helpful, the one he didn't want to write would be a thousand times more important.

He argued against writing a book because, in his opinion, there were far too many books being written and published. Especially books about "Look what I did, you can too." Finally, after years of persuasion, he started.

The real issue was not that there are too many books. It was his own fear of rejection, just like we all feel. Now that he has chosen to start, I can't wait to read it.

Before you get lost in the maze of writing, editing, cover design, publishing, publicity, and marketing, the fundamental choice to make is: "Do you have a desire to serve?"

If that desire is paramount in your heart and you believe that what you have to say will be helpful and make a difference, then the rest of it is just process.

This book will guide you through that process. I cannot create a desire to serve in your heart. That comes from you.

CHAPTER 9

WHAT IT POSSIBLE?

Now that you've come to the place that you know you want to serve and you have something good to share, it is natural to wonder about the options.

Writing a book is only one of many things you can do. With advances in the Internet and communication, it is possible to reach a worldwide audience with any message in a variety of ways.

I briefly mentioned some possibilities earlier, but here is a bigger list in one place of just some of what you can do to spread your message and help those you want to serve:

- Write a book.

- Use your book to create a speaking platform and pursue speaking opportunities.

- Create an online course.

- Partner with others who have a complimentary audience.

- Create a podcast.

- Create a video podcast.

- Create a YouTube channel.

- Create an on-line teaching or coaching workshop.

- Create an in-person teaching or coaching workshop.

- Create products or services that are sold as "do-it-yourself" classes.

- And a dozen variations of each.

- Creating the product is just the start. Then comes marketing and delivery of the products and services you create. There are thousands of courses that teach you:

- How to put together an attractive offer.

- How to market something on the Internet.

- How to speak effectively in public.

- How to teach effectively.

- How to gather a tribe.

- How to pitch a book or idea.

- How to do everything else.

We will cover possibilities and processes more in Part III of the book. For now, the lists above are to get you excited about your alternatives. Undoubtedly you will need help with making your choices happen. That is fine. Help is available.

Internal certainty about your choice to share and clarity about your message is most important here. If you want what you write to have an impact, get clear with yourself about what you want your book or course to do. Answer the simple question: What do you hope will happen?

It doesn't matter how good you are at marketing, copywriting, creating videos, making beautiful websites, speaking, or anything else. What matters first and foremost is that your message is clear, it makes a difference to those who hear it, you know who your audience is and why it will matter to them.

After you have your audience specified, then crafting the message is next. How you do that depends on who the audience is. Where can you reach them? How did they like to consume content? What do they need? Specifically, how will your message help them? Take some time and write down answers to these questions. Time invested now will save mountains of frustration and doubt later.

The purpose of this chapter is not to overwhelm you with the task but to inspire you with the opportunity. There is no reason on earth you can't write a book, create a course, or teach something from your life for the benefit of others and create some wealth for yourself.

The barriers for nearly everyone occur in one of the following three ways. First, lack of clarity about what you want to say, who it helps, and why they benefit. Second, failing to get the right help and third, lack of commitment to see the project through to completion.

This completion includes not only creating the book or other product but includes all the work marketing and delivering the product so that the intended audience gets the benefits.

CHAPTER 10

THE CHOICE

I t's time to decide.

Yes, you have a busy life with lots of other things to do.

Yes, you run the risk that everyone will laugh at you and think you are silly.

Yes, you might do it wrong, or it might fail.

Yes, you might have to do it again and again and again.

Yes, you might be crazy to think you should do this.

Steve Jobs is the one credited with a beautiful quote that contained the following "the ones who are crazy enough to think that they can change the world are the ones who do."

There is no reason this can't be you. You decide what you will do and who you will be. You choose the impact you have on the world.

I don't care what your circumstances are, what your responsibilities are, or what else you have to do. If you feel called to make a difference and writing a book or creating a message in another way is part of that calling, then do it.

Sing the song you came to sing.

Make the choice.

Now.

The rest of this book is going to show you how to do that.

CHAPTER 11

THE NINE QUESTIONS PART 1

When I help people get started with writing a book, creating a course, or some other method of expressing their truth, I start with nine important questions.

1. **Why are YOU writing THIS book NOW?**
2. **Who is the book for?**
3. **When your ideal reader finishes the book, closes the cover and puts it down, what do you want them to do at that moment?**
4. What kind of a book is it?
5. What is the voice of the book?
6. How long do you think the book will be?
7. What research will be involved?
8. After the book is completed, what else are you going to do?
9. How are you planning to publish your work?

We will work through these nine questions in three different chapters. This chapter will deal with the three bolded questions.

Question #1

Why are YOU writing THIS book?

You can read this question in a number of ways. If you simply ask, "Why are you writing this book?" With no emphasis on any word, you will likely answer with a general explanation of what is driving you to tell your story and a vague explanation of what you want as a result.

That is an appropriate answer at the simplest level. Now we go deeper.

The next way to read the question is, "Why are YOU writing this book. This changes the focus a bit and makes you reflect on the driver for you to write this book. Spend some time exploring the difference it makes to ask the question with this emphasis.

A third way is to ask is, "Why are you writing THIS book?" In other words, what drives you to write a book on this topic? Often when someone is writing about their own journey, there is a temptation to write a "different" book. One that is not so personal. Not personal = not powerful. Spend some time with the choice of THIS book until you are certain.

A fourth way is to ask is, "Why are you writing this book NOW?" What are the events, societal conditions, or other drivers that make you believe that this is the moment for your experience and information to be introduced into the marketplace?

All those are important questions. As you prepare to write, you should be able to answer each question without question and hesitation. Why you? Why this topic? Why now? Getting specific about those answers is powerful motivation and clarity as the project moves forward.

Question #2

Who is the book for?

Frequently, this question is treated trivially. People often say, "Well, I think everyone could benefit from reading my book." Bordering on vanity, this answer demonstrates a complete lack of understanding of the power of your message.

A much more effective way to think about this question is, "Who would be the perfect person to read this book?" Framing the question this way forces you to think about the characteristics and needs of a specific person or group of people who would *most* benefit from the book.

Without that specific focus, we tend to write generically with sweeping generalizations and a lack of clear purpose. The result is usually an unimpressive work that is too vague to be of much use to anyone.

You will serve your intended audience far better by getting clear, down to the level of a single person, who you think would be the "ideal reader."

Is it a man or a woman?

How old are they?

How much money do they have or not have?

What trials or struggles have they had in life?

What do they like?

What do they hate?

What is missing most for them?

What is their biggest struggle right now?

These are just a few example questions. As you do this exercise, you should think of at least ten very specific questions that suit your topic and reader. When you do this, and you answer them truthfully, and with some thought, you end up with a single face in front of you.

Now you know exactly who you are writing for. The mark of an effective speech and effective book or an effective marketing campaign is this phrase "Speak to one, talk to many."

Question #3

When your ideal reader finishes the book, closes the cover and puts it down, what do you want them to do at that moment?

It's all well and good to hope they "enjoy" the book. If you are trying to help someone with your experience and want them to benefit from your work, you must have a goal in mind.

In a perfect world, exactly what would they experience at the conclusion of your work? What would you want them to do, right then? Are you prepared to extend an invitation to them to take a specific action because of what you wrote?

Understanding a precise outcome helps you shape the arc of the story through the book and create the instructions you give or requests you make. Knowing this at the start will increase the likelihood of creating the impact you're looking to have.

If you take these first three questions seriously and answer them with care, it will bring a great deal of rigor to the rest of the process. What you want to accomplish will be easy for you to visualize as you tell your story and teach your truth.

CHAPTER 12

TELLING YOUR STORY

In the example of our cab ride at the beginning, the passenger, Candace, was lost in her own thoughts as she got in the cab. The last thing she wanted to do was engage in conversation with the cabbie.

At the same time, it was clear she wanted to go to the opera because she got in the "Opera Express." She had an appointment to meet someone there and attend that performance.

Her state of mind getting in the cab could be described this way:

"I have to go to the opera."

"I don't want to do this."

"I'm unhappy that I'm here."

"Why did I get this stupid assignment?"

"This is going to be really long and boring."

"Why does somebody write the stupid operas anyway?"

"Why did my boss think this was a good place to meet her client?"

Likely you can think of many other things she might be thinking. The thrust of all these is her negative set of assumptions about both the opera, the waste of time, the effectiveness of the venue, and everything else.

She was certainly not planning on getting any instruction from the cab driver and had no expectation or even desire to change her way of being.

At the same time, if she had known it was possible to enjoy the evening, follow the opera story and have a good business meeting, she would have been very interested in what she could do to create that outcome.

The cab driver had two distinct challenges. First, he had to get her attention and pull her out of her inward-facing funk. Second, he had to create a sense of connection so she would be ready to hear anything he said.

You face a similar challenge in writing a book. Even if you are very specific and clear about who needs the book and the benefits they would get from reading and applying your knowledge; the potential reader does not know that yet.

Your first challenge in the book is to pull the reader, even if they aren't quite an ideal target, out of their current mindset and put them in a place of openness. They must believe there is a possibility for them in these pages.

Second, they must also believe that you are the one that could have something for them.

I'm not talking here about the cover, title, sub-title, appearance of the book, or any of those things. We're past that because they already have the book in hand. I'm talking about the first chapters of the book, where you have the opportunity to either connect with or repel the reader.

If you're going to help someone with a challenge, they must first connect with you. I don't care how good your information is, if they don't believe you're speaking the truth or if they think you don't know what you're talking about, they won't be listening as they read.

One of the fastest ways to create an initial connection with someone or establish a rapport is for them to see the two of you share an important experience in your lives.

This is why story matters. You start by telling some part of your story relevant to the topic of the book and the advice you will give.

If you tell a story about yourself that includes situations and circumstances where you have felt like they feel now, you can create rapport and connection.

If they understand you have struggled with the same things or had the same problems or been lost in the same way they currently are, they will likely listen to you.

The key to make this happen is to tell your "developmental story." The next chapters will deal with how to create such a story.

Your developmental story must be interesting and not boring. It must be concise and not contain too much detail or be too long. It must be direct, clear and relevant to both the topic and the reader.

The point in the cabdriver story where that connection was created came at the end of chapter 1. Candace leaned forward in the seat so she could hear the cabbie better. This marked a change in her attitude from "leave me alone," to "maybe there's something here for me."

Your developmental story serves the same purpose. Let's dive into how to do that so your audience will be interested in what you have to say.

CHAPTER 13

DEVELOPMENTAL STORY PART I

All of us experience thousands upon thousands of events during our lifetime. Each shapes us in different ways. Many events have a tiny impact. Small events repeated regularly have a larger impact. Big events can have a dramatic impact, even if they happen only once.

What does all this have to do with creating a "developmental story?"

This series of events that unfolded in your life have brought you where you are today. You have a story to tell and something to teach you that you believe will help those who read it.

There are two parts to this truth. First, the events themselves. They happened, and they affected you. Second, the way you internalized, reacted to, and learn from those events.

It would be difficult and likely boring to tell the whole story. Instead, the key is choosing a set of events that are most relevant to your personal.

We go back to the first question. Why are YOU writing THIS book? If you take some time to reflect, you will be able to find perhaps ten to twenty events that relate both to your topic and your personal development.

Let's say you are writing a book on resilience and our ability to overcome challenges. Reflecting on your life, you will see relevant events that relate to this topic.

For example, perhaps you broke your leg in grade school. Initially, it may have been a big disappointment. You then moved through the healing process, and, it, in fact, healed.

You remember the event like it was yesterday. The pain, the visit to the doctor, putting the cast on, realizing you can't do anything for six weeks, all the kids at school signing your cast and all the rest.

This was a memorable event. You know that because you remember the details and the impact it had on you when it first took place and as it unfolded. This could be a candidate event.

Another event might be that your parents divorced when you were in high school. That is a cataclysm that is all too common in today's families.

You remember like it was yesterday. The growing sense of unease as you knew something was wrong. The looming sense of dread, as you realize something was about to happen.

Finally, hearing from one or both of your parents that they were not staying together. The devastation, blaming yourself, and the rest you recall so clearly.

Then it happened. Then the first year went by. Relationships changed in your family. You discover different friends at school based on your experience.

Again, this is a significant event. You know this because you remember the details, and just thinking about it today brings up a set of feelings associated with all that happened.

Here is the assignment.

Whatever the topic you have chosen, there will be several obvious events in your life that shaped your relationship to that topic.

Take a couple of hours and go for a walk, think about who you are today and how you got here. Think about ten or twenty significant events that had a big impact on creating the person you are today concerning this topic you are teaching.

Ten or twenty is just a suggestion. There is nothing magic about those numbers. Do what makes sense to you and create the list of events.

You can't use every significant event in your life, even though all of them might be peripherally related. The point is to pick the obvious and significant ones that relate to your development with respect to what you plan to teach in your book or course.

Depending on how old you are and what you're writing about, events might start in childhood and go until the present. You may need to do the assignment a few times until you have a list that you think is representative of the events that were formative for you.

When I wrote my book *Tightrope of Depression – My Journey from Darkness, Despair and Death to Light, Love and Life*, my events went all through my life starting in childhood and continuing until just a few years before I began writing. It made sense because I lived with undiagnosed and untreated depression until I was 54.

The key here is to answer the following question in the simplest way possible: "What events in my life shaped how I feel and what I know about the topic I am going to teach in this book or course?"

The first time you make a list will not be perfect. Just get started on making your list. Undoubtedly, you will think of other events and refine your list as you move through the creation of your Story Arc™.

Put the events in chronological order on a piece of paper. Use the example below as a model for a starting point. There is no perfect way to do this, and the example below is just one way to get going.

Developmental Story – Part 1

Event	What Happened	What Did It Do To Me	Why Does This Matter To The Reader
Broke my leg in 3rd grade	Tried to some new stuff on the bars, because my friend did	• Pain, angry at my friend • Mad because I missed a trip	• Learned it eventually heals • Events aren't permanent
Parents got divorced in high-school	Growing anger and tension at home, eventually we had "the talk," and I knew they were divorcing	• Felt abandoned • Blame myself • Felt deprived • Tried to take advantage of my mom being alone – then I got over-protective	• Things happen • I don't control others • I can get through anything • I'm not a victim
I was accepted into College	I was worried I didn't think my grades were good enough	• I realized things have consequences. • I wanted to go back in time.	• There is always a way forward

CHAPTER 14

DEVELOPMENTAL STORY PART II

After you have a list of events you believe shaped your life concerning your topic, we are ready to begin the creation of your story.

In the picture below, you see the second column labeled "What Happened?"

Developmental Story – Part 2

Event	What Happened	What Did It Do To Me	Why Does This Matter To The Reader
Broke my leg in 3rd grade	Tried to some new stuff on the bars, because my friend did	▪ Pain, angry at my friend ▪ Mad because I missed a trip	▪ Learned it eventually heals ▪ Events aren't permanent
Parents got divorced in high-school	Growing anger and tension at home, eventually we had "the talk," and I know they were divorcing	▪ Felt abandoned ▪ Blame myself ▪ Felt deprived ▪ Tried to take advantage of my mom being alone – then I got over-protective	▪ Things happen ▪ I don't control others ▪ I can get through anything ▪ I'm not a victim
I was accepted into College	I was worried I didn't think my grades were good enough	▪ I realized things have consequences ▪ I wanted to go back in time	▪ There is always a way forward

In this column, factually describe what took place. This is not an emotional description; it is to allow you to think clearly about what actually happened.

Doing this thoroughly will help later as you complete column three.

Back to our example in the last chapter. If you decided that breaking your leg in elementary school was one of the significant events that taught you about resilience, then column two could look like this:

"In third grade, I was playing on the gym equipment at recess. I saw one of my friends do something unusual on the parallel bar. Not wanting to be left out, I tried to do it also. I missed putting my leg through my arms and fell down. I landed funny, and it hurt terribly. I tried to stand up and couldn't. I had a broken leg."

That is the basic description of the event. Obviously, the situation continued from there. The teacher was probably called, then came the ambulance, and you went to the hospital.

Perhaps your parents came, and they took you to the doctor. Then there was the healing process and on and on. Pick a boundary between the end of the actual event and the ongoing consequences.

This will become clearer in the next chapter as we fill out the third column on the spreadsheet. For now, take each event that you picked in chapter 13 and write a brief and factual description of what happened.

Remember, this is not the place to write down the emotional consequences or the long-term fallout from what happened. "Just the Facts…"

It is not necessary that the events you choose be negative. In fact, there should be a mix. Perhaps in third grade, you went to Disneyland for the only time during your childhood.

Such an event could be very powerful in a developmental story, depending on why you went and what happened while you were there.

With every event, there will be a question in your mind as to where column two ends and column three begins. Column two is, "What happened?" Column three is, "What did this event do to me?"

Don't get too caught up in getting it "exactly right." For now, just write what happened in column two as a factual statement of the occurrence.

This spreadsheet does not show up in your book. It is a tool for you to create your Story Arc™. After you finish column two for all the events, then go through the two columns again.

With two columns finished, you will see a page or two that list events instrumental in shaping your life related to what you're writing about.

Undoubtedly, writing this will bring up emotions and memories and cause you significant reflection. This is good. If this happens, they were important events, and they contributed significantly to your development.

If you find in doing this second review that you want to change one or more of the events in column one, then do so. Then write the appropriate description in column two.

Again, this process will be iterative through all four columns on the sheet, so don't get caught up in trying to do it "right."

CHAPTER 15

DEVELOPMENTAL STORY PART III

Now that you have a list of appropriate events and a good and succinct description of what happened, you ready to go on to column three.

In this column, your goal is to describe the impact that the event had on you. Unlike where we described the event factually and unemotionally, column three is not limited.

For each event, describe how it felt, what you believed, what changed in your life, and your heart because of that event, not only at that time but as the process unfolded.

Developmental Story – Part 3

Event	What Happened	What Did It Do To Me	Why Does This Matter To The Reader
Broke my leg in 3rd grade	Tried to some new stuff on the bars, because my friend did	• Pain, angry at my friend • Mad because I missed a trip	• Learned it eventually heals • Events aren't permanent
Parents got divorced in high-school	Growing anger and tension at home, eventually we had "the talk," and I know they were divorcing	• Felt abandoned • Blame myself • Felt deprived • Tried to take advantage of my mom being alone – then I got over-protective	• Things happen • I don't control others • I can get through anything • I'm not a victim
I was accepted into College	I was worried I didn't think my grades were good enough	• I realized things have consequences • I wanted to go back in time	• There is always a way forward

Back to our example of the broken leg. Column three is where you would describe the fear you had going to the doctor. You never broke a leg before, and you had no idea what to expect.

Perhaps the pain was overwhelming, and you felt frightened. Perhaps your parent was not very empathetic, and you felt like they didn't care.

Perhaps the doctor or the nurse was very empathetic, and you felt more connected to them. Perhaps you remember fearfully asking how long your leg would be broken.

Maybe you never knew anyone with a broken limb, and you thought the effects would be permanent. Perhaps you were relieved to know that it would heal completely, and in eight weeks, you would be running around again.

Perhaps the bone was set incorrectly and had to be rebroken two years later because you had a permanent limp. Perhaps it never healed well, and to this day, when it gets cold, you feel pain.

Maybe you carried anger about breaking the leg for a long time. Maybe you were mad at your friend because they did a trick on the bars you couldn't do, and that enticed you to try something over your head. Maybe you blame them for your broken leg.

Perhaps you carried anger for the doctor because it didn't heal well, and your leg hurt for years. Perhaps later you realized that those sorts of things happen, and how long and how much it affected you was yours to choose.

This column will be the longest. If these events are significant (they should be, or they wouldn't be on the page), this column will trace the effect of this event over time.

How you felt about it at the time, and the consequences that were imposed on your life felt one way when it happened and changed significantly as life went on.

For example, the events I wrote about in the *Tightrope of Depression*, were traumatic and catastrophic at the time. As time has passed, they have changed in meaning and have been the source of great inspiration and growth.

Events that created staggering resentment and bitterness in me have become lights and beacons that remind me to be grateful and to remember how much goodness there is in the world.

Ongoing consequences of some of my significant events have led me to create powerful relationships. They have completely changed other relationships and, in some cases, ended them.

This third column requires considerable thought and work. Remember, you are tracing the processes of your life that brought you to the place to write THIS book. Don't skimp on the time required.

If you feel strongly enough about your journey writing a book to help others, there will be many events that shaped you. The effects of those events change over time and perhaps become more relevant and powerful as your maturity and experience has grown.

When column three is finished, you now have a powerful framework to create a story. You have traced significant events that shaped who you are and what you believe about this topic at this moment.

As you work through column three, undoubtedly you will change out some of the events. You will realize that you forgot some or that ones you thought you initially chose don't matter all that much.

All that is normal. When you've completed column three, you'll have a solid foundation and a clear understanding of why you are who you are right now and why YOU want to write THIS book to help others with your topic.

CHAPTER 16

DEVELOPMENTAL STORY PART IV

At this point, you are ready to tackle column four. This is the most important column of all. Most storytelling approaches stop after the first three columns. That's why most people don't know how to tell stories in a way that is useful to others.

Regardless of how powerful the events were in shaping your life, remember that you are entering into a relationship with someone else. Your reader needs to see the value *for them* in these events.

Remember, in our cab ride at the beginning of the book; Candace only wanted to pay attention to what the cabbie had to say when she realized they shared a common starting point. Initially, both thought opera was boring and difficult to understand.

When she realized they had something in common, it put her in a mental frame to pay attention to what Bill had to say.

Completing column four is how you create a deep connection with your reader so they are prepared to listen to you as you teach what you know in section two of the book.

Developmental Story – Part 4

Event	What Happened	What Did It Do To Me	Why Does This Matter To The Reader
Broke my leg in 3rd grade	Tried to some new stuff on the bars, because my friend did	• Pain, angry at my friend • Mad because I missed a trip	• Learned it eventually heals • Events aren't permanent
Parents got divorced in high-school	Growing anger and tension at home, eventually we had "the talk," and I know they were divorcing	• Felt abandoned • Blame myself • Felt deprived • Tried to take advantage of my mom being alone – then I got over-protective	• Things happen • I don't control others • I can get through anything • I'm not a victim
I was accepted into College	I was worried I didn't think my grades were good enough	• I realized things have consequences • I wanted to go back in time	• There is always a way forward

Column four is labeled, "Why does this matter to the reader?" Even though you are very clear on how each of these events shaped your life, your reader had a different set of events and a different life.

They may or may not be able to see how this could apply to them. This part is delicate because if you launch into "Professor mode" or start preaching a sermon, you will lose attention and destroy the rapport you have created.

The point of this column is for you to build the bridge. After you understand how the event shaped you, one of two things can happen. 1) you share the event and hope the reader sees value – they build the bridge, or 2) you explain how the value not only applied to you but has been useful in other situations – you build the bridge.

The reader will still have their own interpretation, but you have started the process by thinking more generally about how the lessons you learned might help your reader.

To know this, you will need to make some assumptions about the reader. This is why it is so important to know exactly who you think the ideal reader will be. Question two in Chapter 11 requires you to decide who you're writing for.

That doesn't mean others won't read the book and get benefits. It means you have picked a specific target and are following the rule "speak to one, talk to many." Reflecting on exactly who you are writing for will allow you to see how your experience could benefit them.

In filling out column four, you review how the event impacted you. Then with your specific reader in mind, write down how that same event and learning could benefit your reader.

Remember that this spreadsheet does not go anywhere in the book. This is your preparation so you can find your voice and understand how to tell your story effectively.

The purpose of the developmental story is to create a connection between you and your reader and bring them to the place where they believe they are enough like you that you have something beneficial to tell them.

Go through the entire spreadsheet one event at a time and carefully consider how what you wrote about your own journey in column three will benefit the person you think is most likely to read your book.

Record your thoughts in column four. Obviously, you will not control how anyone interprets or uses your stories or your book. But this thinking process will help you tell your developmental story. It will let you connect powerfully and deeply with your intended reader.

Doing this process repeatedly and thoroughly has helped me refine my developmental story to be very effective. I know this because I get reader feedback where people say they connect deeply with the stories, and their lives are profoundly altered. That means I picked relevant events, told them well and in language that mattered.

Sometimes we tell stories in ways to get the most sympathy or make sure people understand how awful or how wonderful something was. That is the ego talking.

Choosing language that means the most to your intended reader is more effective in creating rapport, maintaining interest, and in preparing the reader for what you share in the rest of the book.

CHAPTER 17

PUTTING IT TOGETHER

When the spreadsheet is complete, review it again. Make sure it contains enough elements and examples, so it's easy to see why YOU are writing THIS book.

It should be clear to anyone (if they could fully understand the spreadsheet) that your experience has brought you to a place of learning, maturity, and capability in this area.

As a reminder, the spreadsheet doesn't go in the book. This chapter will outline how to take the spreadsheet and turn it into the first part of the book.

Here is the guiding principle. Section one of your book has only one purpose. Connect with the reader.

If a person decides to read your book, they have chosen to spend some time creating a relationship with you. They want to know you and want something from you.

Whenever I read a book, I consciously say, "I have decided to spend a couple of hours creating a relationship with this author." I make that choice based on the title/subtitle of the book, the back summary, and looking at the chapter titles.

The first part of your book needs to reward the reader. It should feel right to them that they chose to create a level of rapport and the beginning of that relationship.

They need to feel connected to your purpose and your story and feel like they belong somewhere in this journey. They need to feel like they picked the right book.

As you put your story in the first section of the book, use the spreadsheet as a guide. Your goal is to use experiences and tell enough of your story to allow the reader to feel connected.

If you don't feel you can write about your experiences, you may need some help with the writing process. Don't let that be a barrier. Just start, and get help if you need it, but make it happen. My experience is most people are better than they think.

Think of it as gradually getting to know someone. Remember, in the cab ride, in the beginning; I noted a couple of times that Candace, looking out the window, saw some landmarks.

Think of the story scenes as landmarks. You may want to use the stories you choose in chronological order, or you may choose another order that makes more sense to you. Remember, you are thinking about one single person who is the ideal target for your experience and advice.

This person picked up the book because they are attracted to your title, subtitle and the summary on the back. They probably also looked at the chapter titles, along with names they saw, and the flow was attractive.

When I wrote *Tightrope of Depression*, I told short vignettes, mostly in chronological order, to illustrate how the trajectory of childhood abuse left me in a state of profound depression which lasted most of my adult life.

There were probably other ways to do that. Chronologically won't always be best. Here are some guidelines I can give you about using the elements of your developmental story to introduce yourself to your reader.

First, when you meet someone at a party, you have a dialogue and go back-and-forth. You're able to read body language and see what's going on as you talk together. You get to take turns speaking and listening.

A book is a monologue. They are listening to you talk, even though it is the written word. Your goal is to create a monologue in chapter form that introduces you to the reader through the experiences you had.

The second part of the book is to teach them what you learned on your journey. Since the first part creates rapport, they are in a state of mind more likely to believe what you teach.

Second, use descriptive language. Show, don't tell. Talking about something is less interesting and less powerful than describing the experience.

For example, "I got scared when I heard the noise." Is much weaker than "my heart beat fast, and I felt my knees trembling at the sound in the hallway.

The first sentence tells you I had an emotion and the name of the emotion. The second sentence lets you feel with me the physical sensations that came with the emotion.

Don't get intimidated or lost in this. If you haven't written a lot, this can feel overwhelming. Editors can help with this part.

Third, use short sentences and short paragraphs. This is a relatively modern stylistic development. We have an aversion to dense text and big paragraphs. There is so much information thrown at us so fast that we simply don't read big blocks of text.

You increase the likelihood that someone will read and enjoy your story if you use short sentences, small words, and short paragraphs.

As I said before, this is not a writing course, and I am not trying to teach you to be a writer. You can get an editor that can help with any stylistic issues and problems that show up.

Thoughtfully, just tell your story, using the examples you created on your spreadsheet and remember that you are conducting a monologue to create a relationship with your reader.

CHAPTER 18

THERE IS MAGIC IN STORY

When I help clients write books, I often hear the complaint, "I have nothing interesting to tell." Or said another way, "who would want to read anything about me."

I can't convince you that you have a story worth telling. You need to make that decision by going inside your heart and asking some questions.

"Do I have something I truly believe will help others?"

"Are there people I know who are struggling with the same problems I had and eventually overcame?

"Do I really have a desire to serve?"

These and similar questions will put you in touch with the truth of your purpose. If you have a desire to help and you believe you have something to say, then you should write a book.

Storytelling has been the principal vehicle of communicating tradition, religious values, mythology, and our common humanity, from generation to generation, for thousands of years.

Everybody loves a good story.

A powerful example from film will illustrate the point. When you watch a movie, how often do any of the actors look directly into the camera and speak to the audience?

The answer is "never" unless there is a comedic or other reason to do so. In drama, that is called "breaking the fourth wall." Basically, it never happens.

The actors remain focused on each other and on the scene that is taking place. They never even acknowledge the audience in any way.

That never prevents any member of the audience from identifying with the characters. We regularly sandwich ourselves into the plot, into the character and behaviors of one of the people we see on screen.

We identify strongly with them; we believe we know what they are feeling, and we believe we have had a similar circumstance. We do all this while knowing they are actors, and this is a movie.

Telling your story in a book will be exactly the same except that you are talking about real life, not fiction. If you simply tell the story so I can feel it with you and you help me understand how it benefits me, then I will connect.

Remember, this is not a lecture where you are telling me what to do or trying to get me to see things your way. You are simply telling the story of what happened to shape your life into the person that needs to write this book.

If you do that and simply tell the story, your reader will take care of seeing themselves in your situations and inserting themselves into the plot of your development.

Your developmental story will resonate with their life experience powerfully and effectively. They will develop rapport and kinship with you and will understand what you have been through.

This is true because only people who are attracted to your story will read the book. People that do not resonate with the title, the subtitle, the subject matter, or the chapters will not read the book.

They will continue looking for another book written by someone else that has a story that resonates with them. Those who read your book are attracted and will resonate with you if you follow the directions in preparing and telling your story.

There is magic in the story. By the end of the first part of your book, they will be ready and eager to listen to what you learned and anxious to figure out how it can help them with their own struggles.

PART II

P art two is where you share what you have learned from your life experience and guide the reader on a path where they can also benefit.

The incidents you chose in the spreadsheet were picked because they were important in making you who you are today: the person who needs to write this book.

Here you organize and present your insights and learning, so someone who sees themselves in your situation can avoid heartache and pitfalls because of what you teach.

For example, in *Tightrope of Depression*, I chronicled my journey through decades of undiagnosed and untreated mental illness, then I talked about my recovery and return to normalcy.

After talking about what I had done to get my life straight, I shared many suggestions based on what I learned from things tried. Sharing these things is not intended to be "giving the answer." Nor is it given as a lecture. It is reflective of experimentation and exploring things that work for me.

Because recovery from any mental illness is usually an ongoing process and may never be complete, it's also my current practice to maintain health and healing.

Sharing my journey and the things I'm doing now to stay healthy is my effort to benefit others who might be struggling with the same situation or caring for those who do. Besides, I discovered that the ongoing internal work led me to write a follow-up book titled *Down From the Gallows.*

One way to teach something is by giving a list of principles or actions with examples illustrating how they apply to the subject of your instruction.

You could create the "10 commandments of resilience." That might be fun, and it might be great for quotes on memes. But if all you do is take your stories from part one and hope your reader understands how they apply to them, you will limit your success.

A better way to do this kind of teaching is through a "framework." A framework is a tool that hooks all the ideas you have into a coherent structure.

It will take some work to organize the help you offer. But the work will be amply rewarded in two different ways, both of which are important.

First, you will strengthen and consolidate your own growth. The work of thinking through and organizing what happened to you as you changed your habits and practices will elevate your success and personal growth even further.

Second, it will be far easier to teach those who read your book and simpler for them to remember.

In creating a framework, you might use diagrams, create a lexicon, or make conceptual models that effectively illustrate what you teach.

If you decide that you want to formally teach the contents of your book in classes or workshops, the framework you create will serve you by making that easier to present and sell.

Many clients I have worked with over the years use the Story Arc™ process to write a book about their experience and then launch other products and services to serve clients.

This is easier when you have a good framework. The Story Arc™ is the tool to help you create that framework.

CHAPTER 19

CREATING A FRAMEWORK

In the introduction to this section, I talked about creating a "framework." Let's talk about what that looks like and how to build one for your story.

I will give you a couple of examples of frameworks I created to teach things to clients and sell courses and workshops. If you follow this section carefully, you will find it easy to create a framework from what you have to teach.

One of my frameworks is *The Results Equation*™. I spent many years as a senior executive and consultant in the energy industry. Many of the projects I worked on were difficult and technical.

Some of these projects involved creating software and market platforms that were new to the industry. This required new systems, new thinking, and some serious software programming. This was one of many examples of a successful career in helping people do hard things.

When I became a coach, I wanted to create a framework to explain the principles I used to get these difficult things done. I wrote "The Results Equation™."

The framework in that book is a simple equation, which is why I named the book as I did. The framework is this: UP + ME + CF + CP + RE = Results.

Presenting it as an equation made it feel like "if you do these five things in the right order, then you will get the results you want." Creating that feeling was intentional. Using an equation also made it feel like mathematics. Mathematics is predictable and certain.

All these things together helped create confidence and certainty around the idea that a difficult thing was doable if you just follow the equation.

In that equation, each of the terms stood for one part of the model. For example, UP is an acronym that stands for "Understanding the Present." Before you can make any goal real, you must have a clear understanding of where you are today respecting that goal.

"Understanding the Present" is the process to come to an understanding of where you are starting. If I want to go to Denver, I need to know where I am today so that I can be sure of my direction of travel.

When do I want to be in Denver? If my desire is to be in Denver sometime next month and I am in Miami today, the project looks completely different than if I am in Los Angeles and need to be in Denver tonight.

A travel example is easy to understand, but the principle applies to any project. Understanding the present has several subparts depending on the complexity of the project and the number of people involved. There are steps to make sure you complete that part of the equation successfully.

Each part of the equation has a similar process. Successfully navigating all the steps means you complete your project. After I created the framework, I was able to fill workshops and seminars teaching *The Results Equation*™. It was easy because the framework explained what would happen, and people understood the progression through an equation.

That is one framework I use to make things happen. It works in both business and personal contexts. A framework you create will be completely different based on what you are teaching and what is appropriate to convey the message.

I also teach a seminar on *How to Create Time*. Part of the class refers to tools and techniques we all use. Using calendars wisely, learning to say no, figuring out how to prioritize and a host of others. Because these tools are familiar, I do not include them in the framework for this class.

In the more advanced sections of the class, I introduce things people haven't thought about or heard of. To make that more effective, I use a picture to illustrate techniques of creating time. The picture helps people remember and refer to what we talk about.

That framework is pictured below:

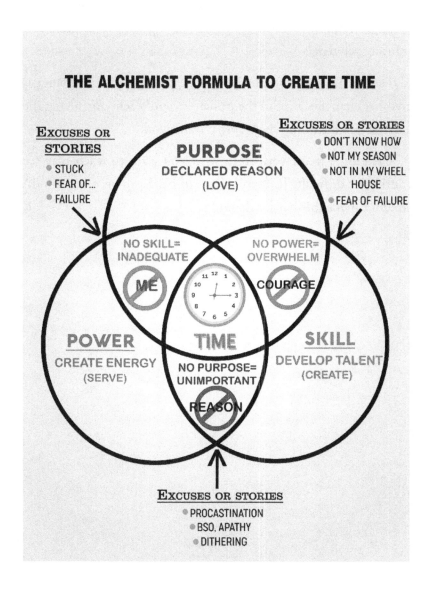

Using a picture makes it easy to explain principles and makes it easy for the reader or workshop participant to understand and remember what's going on. They also take a picture with them to use for future reference.

Part of the story arc process will be creating pictures, language, and other elements around the principles you teach, organizing them effectively, and turning them into a framework.

Creating a framework from what you want to teach may seem daunting or difficult. It doesn't have to be. Keep an open mind, so you don't make this harder than it is.

CHAPTER 20

IF YOU HAD CONTROL...

Life often happens in haphazard ways. Sometimes we look back and see there was a method to the madness, but usually, in the moment, it all seems very random.

My raging struggle through the battlefield of depression, addictions, ruined relationships, and health challenges did not seem organized or helpful in any way.

Because I wandered through life, reacting to circumstances around me, and struggling with unknown monsters in my head, things did not happen in a pretty or organized fashion.

Thinking about it later, it was possible to put the learnings in some semblance of order. When I sat down to write *Tightrope of Depression*, I was able to see some threads that had been consistent through my struggles and recovery.

I made a list of things I learned. Using the fourth column in the spreadsheet, I extracted an outline of truths about life, learnings about myself, and discoveries about the way the world works.

Then I organized those learnings.

It is not very effective to teach something randomly. For example, when I learned calculus in college, I needed some background. If I know some geometry and trigonometry, then I'm prepared with the tools to begin the study of calculus.

Because you have come to a point where you are choosing to write a book and describe the journey you made, two things are clear: First, you have had a set of experiences that have brought you to a new level of awakening.

Second, you see those experiences taught you truths, principles, and techniques that might have helped you, and you believe it could help someone else. With the benefit of hindsight, which you now have, you are in a position to organize this learning.

Others that are in your situation or have similar circumstances will likely also feel they have been through a haphazard and random life flow. Learning the framework you create is the organization they need.

One way to think about this organization is to ask the question, "if I had to do it all over again, is there order and a sequence to how a person could learn these things?"

Based on what you have now learned, what should be first to be most effective? In *The Results Equation*™, the first step is knowing where you are now. It is necessary to understand where you are before you can create any kind of a path to a goal.

Therefore, UP or Understanding the Present is the place to start. It doesn't matter what the goal is, and it doesn't matter where you're going, you must understand where you are to begin.

Examining the principles you teach based on your life learnings and your experiences is much the same. Looking over the learnings from column four of the spreadsheet will give you the basic elements to create a path through your teaching.

Here are some questions that might help.

- What is the first thing I need to know before the rest makes sense?
- Why don't I already know that?
- What are the barriers and beliefs that keep me in the dark?
- What are the first steps to help my learning?
- How can I anchor this learning to my present experience?
- What things need to change for me to remember and apply this principle?

These and similar questions will help you not only identify the path through the teaching you want to give; it will also provide you an instructional framework to help your reader learn.

Remember, we decided the person most likely to read your book would be one who had some similar life experiences to yours. They would recognize your trials and struggles and be enlightened by your discoveries.

As you do this, it is critical to remember, "speak to one, talk to many." As you tell the story and gather and organize the lessons you want to teach, you are speaking to one person.

Don't worry about getting it "right" just yet. You will have plenty of opportunities to refine the language and make sure you have done your best as you write and edit later.

When you finish this process, you will have three to seven learnings that constitute the core of what you want to teach. Each one may have subparts, to make it logical and memorable.

Using the spreadsheet from part one and this list of principles you create from column four, you are getting the elements in place to create your Story Arc™.

CHAPTER 21

USE PICTURES

A picture is worth a thousand words. That adage is as true in teaching your framework as it is in photography and filmmaking.

As you create the list of principles with subparts, you want to teach and organize them in order, think about how to represent them with pictures.

They don't have to be photographs. They can be stick drawings or clip art or hand drawings you create yourself. It doesn't matter.

What matters is that you believe the picture or drawing you are using is powerfully tied to the principle. Referring to the pictures during your teaching in part of your book will help the reader anchor what you say and remember it later.

In the various books I have used:

- Venn diagrams.

- Photographs.

- Hand drawings.

- Clipart.

- Graphs.

Anything is fair game. If it's humorous, it increases impact. In one version of *The Results Equation*™, I used a picture of the abominable snowman.

I said something funny about it in the text. It became a hallmark of workshops I taught because people remembered the picture of the abominable snowman.

Make sure that you check copyrights, so you don't get in trouble with what you use. If you pay an artist to create illustrations, make sure you have the right to reproduce them.

If you take your own photographs, then obviously there's no problem. If you use drawings you have made, you own that creative output.

Be wildly creative. If they're funny, that's a plus. The more memorable, the better. This is a place where you can let your imagination run wild.

I have never had a client show me an illustration or picture so outrageous I thought it should be omitted from the book.

Remember, at this stage, you are assembling resources to teach your principles, make an impact, and benefit your readers. You can choose to leave things out later, so don't worry too much about any editing at this point.

CHAPTER 22

CREATE YOUR FRAMEWORK

Now the rubber meets the road. You have a list of principles and associated subparts. You have a collection of pictures, illustrations, and drawings that emphasize and demonstrate your thoughts.

It's time to create your framework. Let's make this easy. Remember, a framework is just an organizational tool to assist in presenting your ideas and making them memorable.

A Framework can be a list, a diagram, an acronym, a model, or anything else that gives an anchor to remember and apply what you are teaching.

For example, here are some of the frameworks I have created.

These two examples are from *Walking Without Fear.*

This first one I called "The Surrender Trail,' or "The Line of Learning."

Surrender ----------> Peace -----------> Joy -----------> Purpose -----------> Power

This is called "The Four Threads of Life."

The Thread of Connectedness

Alone — Connected — United

The Thread of Freedom

Trapped — Free — At Cause

The Thread of Freedom

Not Good Enough — Powerful — Unstoppable

The Thread of Freedom

Worthless — Important — Precious

From *Meeting God at the Door*, these are the "Four Eternal Truths" I learned during one of my visits with God.

   o Each of us is divine and an intentional child of God.

   o Each of us has divine potential and a mission or purpose in this world.

   o Each of us has gifts and talents given us to accomplish that purpose.

   o All the help needed to accomplish that purpose and live to our fullest potential is available from both infinite sources and in the world around us.

In Chapter 19, I listed a couple of others as well.

You know from your own experience other frameworks.

- The Ten Commandments.

- The Golden Rule.

- Karma Payback.

These are all associated with spirituality, but there are hundreds associated with everyday life, including business and making money. For example:

- The Urgent/Important matrix from Stephen Covey's *7 Habits of Highly Effective People.*
- The 7S framework from McKinsey.
- The AIDA business model from the 1800s.
- The "MBTI Personality Type" from Myers-Briggs.

You may worry it's impossible to create a world-class framework like those listed above. I didn't expect to, and perhaps you won't either.

That is not the point. The point is to create something that helps the reader internalize and execute on what you teach. Creating something memorable and fun is the key.

Don't shy away from this effort. Go at it with an open-heart and a wild imagination.

CHAPTER 23

THE NINE QUESTIONS PART II

In chapter 11, we dealt with the first three of the nine questions. Here they are again. In this chapter, we will deal with the next group as you prepare to create your Story Arc™.

1. Why are YOU writing THIS book NOW?
2. Who is the book for?
3. When your ideal reader finishes the book, closes the cover and puts it down, what do you want them to do at that moment?
4. **What kind of a book is it?**
5. **What is the voice of the book?**
6. **How long do you think the book will be?**
7. **What research will be involved?**
8. After the book is completed, what else are you going to do?
9. How are you planning to publish your work?

Question #4

What kind of book is it?

This is not a trick question. A book has pages and words. Of course, so will your book. It will likely have pictures and frameworks as well.

This question is a very specific one and will have a lot to do with how you create your book. Some books are meant to read from start to finish. There is no need to stop in the middle and do anything.

Meeting God at the Door, was such a book. So was *Tightrope of Depression*. Those were written to tell a story as well as teach some essential principles. My design in those books was to have the learning take place in the mind of the reader as they read along.

Some books are written to be more interactive. For example, *The Results Equation*™ is to invite the reader to participate in actions during the reading.

Some of the chapters have spaces for the reader to fill in after reflection. Instructions are given in the chapter, and there is an opportunity for the reader to compose answers that apply to their situation.

This book is written the same way. You have instructions about creating a spreadsheet and a list of principles which I encourage you to do as you read through the book.

Some books are written to take longer to complete. For example, you may get an assignment in a given book and need to practice that activity for an entire week before you go on to the next chapter.

I took a sales seminar where each chapter was an exercise. I went and implemented the things suggested in that chapter and worked on different conversational techniques for a week.

The following chapter assumed I did that and built upon the principles taught to expand my skill at creating relationships for sales.

Depending on how you intend to teach and your reader to implement, you'll decide what kind of book you are going to write.

How will the reader interact with your content?

I read another book with video links inside. In most chapters, there were links where to watch a video. Some of these videos were 10 or 15 minutes, and some were two hours.

The design of that book was to create an immersive experience during the reading by adding different media and by hearing comments and conversations of others participating in the curriculum.

There is no "right" way to do this. You just need to decide what makes sense for your book. This decision is not unchangeable. Make an initial decision and then review it as you go forward

Question #5

What is the voice of the book?

The voice usually means the pronoun. Since your book is principally about your story, it is most common to be in the first person singular.

It is possible to write a narrative in the third person. This is more like a reporter describing the events as they are witnessed instead of the person experiencing them.

Again, there's no rule about this. If you narrate in the third person, you must make sure you have the skill to keep the reader clear about who's talking and what's going on, so they don't get lost in the story.

If this is your first book and you're telling your own story to teach principles you have learned, I would recommend writing in the first person singular.

Question #6

How long do you think the book will be?

When I asked this question, people often say, "I have no idea." I understand that. After you have the spreadsheet completed from part one and the principles you'll teach in part two, you'll have an idea about how many chapters you expect.

It is useful to go to the bookstore and look at other books that talk about something like your work. Find several that cover similar topics. Don't worry. This is not an exercise in discouragement.

There will never be too many books written. No matter how many books have been written about your topic, someone needs to hear it in your voice.

The purpose of going to the bookstore is to get an idea of the size of the book that you might write. Look through several books that contain stories about the author and teach something useful to the reader.

You can get a rough word count by counting the words on a few lines and then averaging them. Multiply that by lines on a page. Then multiply by pages in the book. It won't be perfect, but you will get an idea.

Some examples from my books, *Walking Without Fear,* is 39,000 words. *Tight rope of Depression,* is 68,000 words. *Meeting God at the Door* is 33,000 words. This book is about 41,000 words.

Looking at those books will give you an idea of how long your book might be.

This number is not a limit on how many words you can write or a goal about what you should do. It's to give you an idea of how big the project is. As you plan your writing, this will be important.

When you start writing, after a few hours of work, you will get a sense of how many words you write per hour. Then you can figure out how long it will take you to write the first draft. This is helpful to keep you from getting discouraged and frustrated when things get a little difficult.

Question #7

What research will be required?

If you are writing a story about your own experience and what you learned, you may not need to do any research. You are simply describing your experience and thoughts.

On the other hand, you may want to research current thinking is about the topic you address.

For example, when I wrote *Tightrope of Depression*, I read dozens of books on depression to see what others had to say. I also read dozens of medical articles to understand what current thinking was.

This helped me frame my own thoughts and express my advice in the context of what else was going on in the world of depression and those who were writing about it.

When I wrote my five-volume series on meditation, I read books by meditation practitioners, teachers, university scholars, as well as monks and yogis. This was to make sure I could frame my work in a current context at the same time as describing my own experience.

This question is not to imply you need research or that researched books are better. This question is designed to help you with planning your work.

Questions #6 and #7 are both aids to help you understand the scope of your project. With a good assessment of what you plan to do with the book, how long it will be, and what research is required, you can make an effective plan to get the book done.

If you have external deadlines or external events like a speaking tour or a product deadline for online marketing, knowing these things is important to help plan and stay on schedule.

CHAPTER 24

DRAW THE ARC

You may be wondering when we're actually going to draw something. The answer is, Now! This is the chapter where you draw your first Story Arc™.

You have assembled the tools and done the work to start this part of the process.

Let's get on it.

The first thing to think about is the pot of gold. Yes, the pot of gold. Think of a rainbow. We all know what we find at the end of the rainbow, right? That beautiful pot of gold.

Start with a piece of paper in landscape mode. Don't worry about fitting everything in. You will do it several times. After you get started, you're going to find you want a much larger piece of paper.

Don't worry about doing anything "right." Just start, and you will figure out what you need as you go along. Draw an arc or rainbow on the piece of paper. That's it.

Story Arc™

Now that you have your first arc drawn, let's populate it. The arc represents the journey of your reader. Think of the cab ride in the first three chapters.

Candace got in the cab at the left end of the arc. She went on a ride for half an hour. She had a conversation with Bill, the cabbie, and got out of the cab at the other end of the arc.

Something happened to her between one end and the other end of the arc. She was changed in that process.

The arc on your piece of paper represents the journey of your reader from the beginning of the book to the end of your book.

If you work your magic, they will be different when they finish. They will start the journey in your book (in your cab) at the left end of the arc, and when your reader finishes the book (gets out of the cab) at the other end of the arc, in some way, they will be changed.

The purpose of this book and the design of the Story Arc™ is to help you craft that journey, so you have the greatest possibility of having the desired effect on your reader.

The pot of gold is at the right end of the arc. If you tell the story well and the reader gets significant benefits from what you teach, they will have discovered that pot of gold.

There is a big difference between "information" and "transformation." We read lots of books and lots of articles in magazines and online and acquire "information."

That's interesting but not powerful. The information doesn't become useful to us unless something changes about how we think, how we act, or who we are. Our goal is to create transformation for the reader, so they experience a difference because they read the book.

Candace had a completely different attitude about the opera, was looking forward to meeting the client, and was ready to provide a great experience for him because of what took place on the cab ride. She had a level of transformation.

I use the rainbow as the metaphor for several reasons. First, there is a pot of gold at the end of the rainbow, right? Second, a rainbow is beautiful. The transformation provided by your story and your teaching is also beautiful.

We will create markers along the arc. They are like the landmarks Candace saw on her journey. As we create the markers along the arc, always remember this question: "Where is my reader on the Story Arc™? What is their experience so far, and what are they feeling now?"

We never really control what someone feels, and you will never know exactly how anyone understands or interprets your book. That's fine. Remember our rule of "speaking to one, talking to many."

If you write your story and teach your message the most powerful way possible for the one person you have in mind, it will be accessible to more people. Again, remember how movies draw us in even though there is no interaction between the actors and the audience. Your story can be exactly the same.

Readers that are part of your tribe will have no problem fitting themselves into the narrative and seeing their situations in your story and teaching.

CHAPTER 25

STARTING CHARACTERISTICS

A t this point, you're ready to start populating the arc. At the left end, make a list of the characteristics of the person who is your ideal reader.

What are they feeling? What is going on in their life right now? What problems are they facing? What have they likely tried? What would they give anything to change?

Think of the example at the beginning of the book. Candace was self-absorbed, frustrated, impatient with the potential waste of time, hoping the cabbie would be quiet, perhaps angry at her boss, and wondering how fast the night could go by.

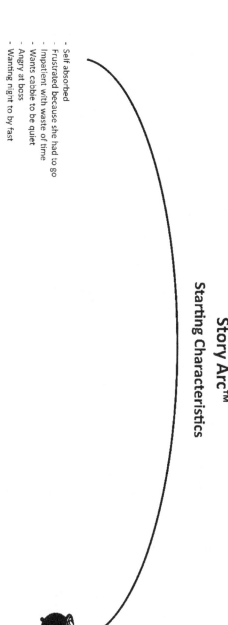

Story Arc™
Starting Characteristics

- Self absorbed
- Frustrated because she had to go
- Impatient with waste of time
- Wants cabbie to be quiet
- Angry at boss
- Wanting night to by fast

In the diagram, you can see I listed all those at the left end of the arc. This list represents your best guess as to the characteristics and feelings of the ideal reader you have in mind.

You might wonder how it's possible to be very accurate about what someone else is feeling. You probably know more than you think you do about their state of mind.

Remember, the reason YOU decided to write THIS book is because you have a set of experiences, events, and learnings that relate to this topic.

Your ideal reader is very likely someone exactly like you were at a previous time in your life. Given that truth, it's highly likely that you will have a good idea of what they are feeling.

My experience is that almost without fail, people I talk to about their lives regularly express the same frustrations, fears, and feelings that I had at an earlier date in my life.

This is not to say that every person you meet in a grocery store is going to spill their guts. They won't. But if you are talking to a person who will be helped by your book because you both have experienced similar circumstances, you will know ahead of time what they're going to say.

They picked up your book and chose to read it because whatever you said in the title, subtitle, description on the back, and in the chapter titles gave them the sense you are a kindred spirit.

Candace came out of the train station and headed directly to the cab in the story because it said "Opera Express." The title, subtitle, and description of your book functions exactly the same way.

You have put up a flag and issued an invitation to that person to read your book. You have given them the hope that you have something to say that might help them with their situation. If your invitation is well constructed, they will be attracted.

Don't complete this step too fast.

Take time to think about the specific problems they are facing, the state of mind they are likely in, and the excuses and stories likely keeping them stuck where they are.

You will be familiar with those. You will recognize them as the same broken record that played through your mind and heart at an earlier time in life.

Don't be afraid to make assumptions here. You are writing the book addressing someone who feels those things and is imprisoned by those beliefs and stories.

You know what the beliefs are, and you know the thought processes and struggles you went through to change yours. You have a great deal to offer your reader.

I had a thousand reasons why I would never write a book. I couldn't imagine being an author or having anything useful to say. I was full of beliefs that made it impossible for me to write a book.

Then, things happened to me, and I changed my beliefs. Then I wrote a book; then I wrote more books. *The Book of Context* is written as an entire course on how to change those beliefs.

All of this is simply to say, take some time and think about the beliefs and barriers of your ideal reader and write them down at the left end of the arc.

CHAPTER 26
WHO ARE YOU TALKING TO?

From the beginning of this book, we have talked about writing to one person. There are several ways you could think about this direction, and some are more productive than others.

For example, when I wrote *Tightrope of Depression*, I could have been writing to "people who have depression." While that might sound reasonable, it wouldn't have helped me write a good book.

During my research, I read many books, articles, and medical reviews about clinical depression, creative people with depression, depression diagnosis and treatment, and other topics. Even with all that, what I knew about the topic, was just a drop in the bucket.

If I wrote to "those who have depression," I would have been continually struggling to find the right words. I would be wondering if the words and examples addressed "people with depression."

Instead, I just told my story to one person. It reflected my journey, starting as a child, through harsh abuse, internal turmoil, religious fanaticism, and the effects those things had on me.

I focused on one face and told the story, one scene, and one memory at a time. Because I created a Story Arc™ and did the work ahead of time to pick the scenes, it flowed easily.

I spoke of childhood events, adolescent apocalypse, epiphanies that portended future change, and ultimately of a total meltdown and divine intervention that completely changed my game. It worked and pawned more books, created courses, and provided clients for my work.

For example, if you had an abusive relationship and wrote your story, it won't be helpful if you write to "those who have been in an abusive relationship."

If that was an important developmental piece of your story, then writing to a single person will be far more engaging and powerful.

Then when you come to the second part of the book and have something to teach, you will have the full attention and engagement of the reader.

If this is your first book or you are dealing with a personal story that includes difficult parts, this will take some practice. You will be tempted to generalize or gloss over important things in the story.

Consider, for example, something as seemingly mundane as gardening. You could simply write a book of gardening tips that you have accumulated over the years.

If, on the other hand, you write a story where part one of the book describes how you came to be a master gardener, you've created a relationship with others who feel the same. You may write about the peace and tranquility you feel when your hands are dirty, combined with the unbridled joy you feel as you view the beautiful flowers.

Then, if you teach how to accomplish this masterful creation in part two of the book, the level of connection, enthusiasm, and the likelihood of follow-through is much higher.

Whatever it takes for you to practice talking to a single person will be worth the effort in the end because of the increased power of your story and teaching.

Pick the person carefully and get to know them even if they are someone you imagine. Be specific about their characteristics and attitudes. Using someone you know may be easier or harder, depending on the person and your relationship to them.

However you make it happen; take the effort and time to create or pinpoint a single person you tell your story to. Then share with them your precious learning.

CHAPTER 27

ENDING CHARACTERISTICS

At the left end of your arc, you listed the characteristics of the person starting the journey through your book or course.

At the other end of the arc (right side) is the pot of gold, which represents the benefit to both you, the writer, and the reader for taking this journey.

Your benefit to you is that you've successfully guided someone through a story and the learning process to benefit their life in ways you can't imagine.

The benefit to the reader is that things have changed in their mind and heart. They are now connected with another person who shared their experience. They have gained valuable insight and suggestions for action.

At the right end of the arc:

Story Arc™
Ending Characteristics

- Self absorbed
- Frustrated because she had to go
- Impatient with waste of time
- Wants cabbie to be quiet
- Angry at boss
- Wanting night to by fast

- Optimistic
- Looking forward to teach my client
- Expecting to enjoy opera
- Thinking about attending more operas
- Grateful to boss
- High expectations for the business deal

Make a list of characteristics of the person who's at the end of your book (when they get out of the cab at the destination).

If we were to imagine such a list for Candace, her characteristics when she stepped out of the cab at the opera house might include:

- Optimistic about the evening.
- Looking forward to teaching the client.
- Expecting to enjoy the opera. Thinking about attending more operas.
- Grateful to her boss for the assignment.
- High expectations for the business deal.

The change took place because of the conversation during the cab ride. The analogy is that there will be a change in your reader as they journey through the book.

The reader chose to have a relationship with you because they read the book. During that relationship, you established a connection by sharing your story.

That connection allows you to be a trusted advisor in the context of sharing learnings with them to benefit their current situation.

When you think about the opportunity to influence someone, it will be easy to specify the characteristics, attitudes, and feelings of the person who reads the book, sits for a moment lost in thought at the conclusion, and then carefully closes the book and puts it down.

What do you want them to feel? What possibilities do you want them to see? What do you hope they choose to do?

This list at the end of the are or rainbow (the pot of gold) is the goal you have for the reader. It's your ideal outcome.

Obviously, people will read a book and think whatever they want. They will interpret the stories how ever they interpret them. The teachings you share will do whatever they do.

Even with that, careful consideration of what you want will allow you to present your story and teaching with the most clarity and the most opportunity to make a difference.

Take some time right now on your Story Arc™ and write the characteristics, attitudes, and intentions of the carefully chosen reader who finishes your book.

CHAPTER 28

ROAD SIGNS OF CHANGE

On the cab ride from the train station to the opera house, Candace noted a few physical things. The train station itself, the sign on the cab, the complicated six-point intersection, the public library, and so forth.

In any journey from one place to another, there are always intermediate markers.

For example, when my wife and I lived in Phoenix, we drove back and forth between Phoenix and Edmonton, Alberta, many times over nine years. Sometimes we made the trip in two long, arduous days but most often we took three.

There were gas stations, restaurants, and motels that were the markers of our journey. When we passed certain landmarks, we knew not only what town we were in but how many hours were left in our trip. It was a visceral feeling, far more than just the name of the town.

taking your reader along the trip of your story, and through your teaching, similar things will happen. At the left end, you have the characteristics at the start. At the right end, you listed the characteristics after the trip. Along the way, certain things will change just like they did in the attitude Candace had toward the opera.

The landmarks in the drive from the train station to the opera house come in a particular order. The complicated intersection was first, then the public library, and so on. You can't rearrange the city.

The journey of your reader will be the same. There will be an order of events for gradual change to help them move from where they start to where they will end.

For example, it's common for people to feel lonely. Like maybe they are the only person in the world facing the problems they have. One notable landmark that is almost always near the beginning of the trip is the realization, "I'm not alone."

Another regular and significant change people experience near the start is the realization, "it's not hopeless; there is something I can do."

Another real source of power along the transformational journey is an actual internal realization "it's not too late." Often people feel like their opportunities have passed, and whatever broke, can no longer be fixed.

Figuring out what the milestones along the way for your reader, is one of the most important exercises you can do while creating your "Story Arc™".

This milestone creation process will be iterative and will take work. It might be helpful to reflect on your journey and consider your development to see what changes had to happen for you before you made progress.

Put them in the order that you think will make things the easiest. It rarely happens in the ideal order in real life, or at least it doesn't seem to, but we should present them in a logical sequence anyway.

Your assignment at this point is to take the arc and write in between the left and the right end. Write ten or twenty gradual change markers that need to happen in your reader. These are like the landmarks a passenger would see between the start and end of their cab ride.

When this is complete, look at your story arc and visualize your reader. See them in their state of mind at the beginning and follow them along through the gradual changes that take place in your book.

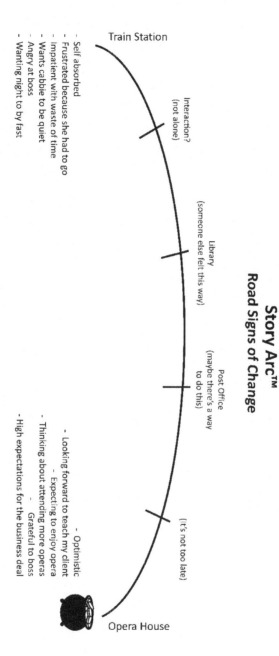

Story Arc™
Road Signs of Change

Train Station

- Self absorbed
- Frustrated because she had to go
- Impatient with waste of time
- Wants cabbie to be quiet
- Angry at boss
- Wanting night to by fast

Interaction?
(not alone)

Library
(someone else felt this way)

Post Office
(maybe there's a way
to do this)

(It's not too late)

- Optimistic
- Looking forward to teach my client
- Expecting to enjoy opera
- Thinking about attending more operas
- Grateful to boss
- High expectations for the business deal

Opera House

See if you can experience the gradual adjustment in their attitude and confidence in mastering their current situation. At the right end of the arc (or the end of the book), they should be in the place described in your "pot of gold."

It will take several times through the story arc to get a set of markers that satisfy you. It doesn't have to be perfect, and you don't have to cover every single change. It just needs to feel like you have a reasonable and logical emotional flow from one end to the other.

Chapter 29

Follow the Path

The next step isn't really a step at all but a caution and guide for how you continue the whole journey through writing the book.

Even though we haven't started writing yet, I'm putting this warning at this stage in the instructions because it needs to guide your thinking from this point forward.

A few months ago, my wife Joy and I were in San Miguel de Allende, Mexico, and we were being driven from the airport along with some other passengers to our various destinations in the city.

San Miguel de Allende is an old colonial city and built in a hilly part of central Mexico. It was night, and we couldn't see much beyond the houses which crowded the street and stood side-by-side.

ome streets were so narrow they had warning signs to make sure no large vehicles entered. We were in a van, and at one point, the driver had to get out and pull the mirrors in. You get the idea.

We turned here and turned there, up steep grades and down scary hills. As we got deeper into the city, I remarked to Joy, "this can't possibly be the shortest way to get to whatever hotel these people are staying at."

There was no reason in the world for the cabbie to take the long way because the fare was fixed, and it would just be a waste of time, but the twists and turns felt confusing and like it couldn't possibly be the best way. Eventually, we completed the trip, and all was well.

You have likely taken a cab ride where you had the sense the cabbie may have been padding the fare by driving around in circles or taking the long way to your destination. That feeling comes because you don't know the way.

Similarly, when you start telling your developmental story, even if you've done the planning with the spreadsheet and some good thinking about it, you will be tempted to jump all over the place.

esist that temptation and remember to "follow the path." This is a critical piece of advice that will keep you from getting discouraged as you write and will help your reader follow through.

This is the reason you do the preparatory work before you do any writing at all. Pick the elements of your story, put them in an order that makes sense, and equate them to the landmarks along the way of your story arc.

The same thing is true with your teaching. Create a logical flow through what you want to share. Put it in order and then stick to the path you create.

The story arc represents the entire journey. The first part of the story arc contains the elements of your story. The purpose here is to establish a connection and rapport with the reader.

The second part of the story arc is your teaching. After they are in a receptive frame of mind, the things you have to teach them will make sense and will be easy to accept if you stick to your path.

The third part of the arc consists of examples of success and encouragement, covered in part three of this book.

All the work that you do in preparation to tell your story and in preparation to present the things you learned will be amply rewarded as you follow the instruction to "follow the path."In the remaining hapters of part two, we will focus on how to present your learnings in an organized fashion, so they follow from the story about your own journey.

Doing the work ahead of time, completing your story arc, and then resisting the temptation to jump around makes the process of writing easy.

ust like a good movie, it has to have a flow. If it jumps around too much, and you can't follow the plot, the timeline, or the character development, it's confusing and unsatisfying.

The same will be true for your book.

Follow the path.

CHAPTER 30

CHAPTER TITLES

In previous chapters, I likened reading a book to creating a relationship with an author. I talked about looking at the title, subtitle, description on the back, and the chapter titles as the obvious and easy way to see if a book appeals to you.

Now that you've created your developmental story matrix and a story arc, with a description of your reader at the beginning of the book, the specific changes that take place along the way, leading to their state of mind at the end, you are ready to create chapter titles.

Chapter titles serve as both an enticement to read the book and an explanation of what to expect along the way.

Using the spreadsheet of your developmental story, especially the columns about what happened in each event and the benefit to the reader, plus the milestones along the arc that guide the reader journey, create a series of chapter titles that tell a story.

This is a mouthful. Let's break it down one step at a time. If you end up with 15 events in your life you believe were significant in helping you move from a place of struggle to a place of effectiveness and joy, you might have 15 chapters in part one of your book.

It's unnecessary to end up with a one-to-one match between events, learnings, and chapter titles. It might be a helpful place to start. Later in the book, we'll talk about chapter length and readability.

We then organize your teaching (using a framework) into key principles. Let's say there are five key principles. Let's assume each principle has two or three subparts. You might have 10 or 15 chapters in part two.

This is an example for illustration. It is not a rule. The key is to think about the journey. The first part creates connection, and the chapters follow you through your developmental journey from struggle to a place of joy and peace.

The second part presents the learnings you have accumulated and teaches them in a framework that lets the reader understand what you learned and how that framework might help.

To start, assign a chapter title to each event and each learning. You can refine it from there.

So far, we have only dealt with the first two parts of the book. As mentioned in chapter 29, the third part of this book will show you how to use your story and your framework to create the biggest impact in the world around you.

Chapter Titles

Section 1 – Story	Section 2 – Teaching	Section 3 - Examples
I broke my leg	- Things happen for a reason	- I worked at my kids school
	- I am my own master	- I fixed a troubled work relationship
	- Take time to reflect	- Etc, etc, etc
	- Don't blame others	
My parents got divorced	- Etc, etc, etc	
I got accepted		
My girlfriend broke my heart		
I got caught cheating		
I graduated		

Like parts one and two, part three will also have chapter titles. We'll do those later. Our goal right now is to take what you have done and craft a set of chapter titles for parts one and two that feel good as a guide to lead your reader through the journey.

Now let's talk about the actual chapter names. There are many ways to name chapters. One way is to simply use numbers. Another way is to be descriptive about the contents.

For example, when I was a young boy, my mom sometimes read to us. Some books she read were written in a style where chapter titles were extraordinarily descriptive.

The chapter title might be two or three sentences long and described in brief everything we could expect to take place in the chapter. That is not in vogue today.

Keep your chapter titles short—one to six words in most cases. If you want examples, you can use the chapter titles in this book or in any of my other books as examples. If you find another style that better suits your content, use it.

I name chapters in a flow to give a person reading the table of contents a sense of how the story progresses through the book. I want them to know what to expect if they choose to spend some time in the pages with me.

Your assignment right now is to take your spreadsheet, your principles, and the markers you have on your story arc and create a flow of chapters for the first two parts of your book.

Don't worry about how many chapters there are. You can have 50 chapters if you want to. What matters more than the number of chapters is how the flow feels to you as you read the chapter titles in succession.

Chapter 31

Three Ideas Per Chapter

There is something magical about the number three. It shows up everywhere. Learning and memorization processes also use the number three. It's even sometimes spoken of as "the rule of three."

It's easy to remember "this, this and that." There is another common legend that odd numbers are more attractive than even numbers. We're not talking about marketing and persuasion here, so we'll just leave it at that.

The chapter title "Three Ideas Per Chapter" is a starting point. There is nothing ironclad about this "rule," but let's use it to get started.

After you have the chapter titles organized and they flow well for you, it's time to decide more specifically what you will write in each chapter.

Let's start with the events you described from your developmental story in part one. One example I used was breaking your leg in elementary school.

The chapter title might my "My Broken Leg." To help write it, think of three things about the event that matters to you in telling the story and framing your learning. For example, the three ideas for that chapter might be: 1) I broke my leg and didn't die. 2) it wrecked some things I had planned to do, and I was devastated. 3) eventually, it healed, and things mostly got back to normal.

This might be a good way to both describe the event and remember the learning. The "return to normal" part might apply to your reader by helping them see some struggle in life isn't permanent. The idea that things heal could be an important principle in your framework.

The chapter on breaking your leg doesn't need to include all the teaching about things that heal. There are probably other events in your story that also make that point in different ways.

It includes three essential points that you want to make about that event. Cover enough, so you fulfill the reason you included it in the final version of your developmental story.

Sometimes, when you are writing down the important things related to an event, you end up with five or six or more critical things you think matter. That is fine. Some things in life are like that.

If that happened, you might consider splitting the chapter. In chapter 32, we'll talk about chapter length and how that relates to readability and flow.

Go through each chapter you have picked for part one and part two of your book and identify three (or more) significant things you want to teach in that chapter.

All this writing will not fit on your story arc page. I use a separate piece of paper for the chapter titles. As you see in the diagram, there are three columns, one for each part of the book.

Then I use another piece of paper to write important ideas for each chapter.

In doing this exercise, you will make some changes. You may decide two events in your developmental story are too similar. You might decide to leave one out depending on what the events are and how closely spaced they are in time, or you might combine them into a single chapter.

After you write the three ideas you want to teach from each incident on paper, it's easier to see overlaps and redundancies.

This observation is particularly true for your framework. However, with a framework, my experience is that rather than redundancies, I generally identify gaps. What seemed like a complete framework to start with, sometimes feels incomplete when I write down the key points for each chapter.

As you choose three crucial points for each chapter of your framework, don't hesitate to make revisions, additions, consolidations, and adjustments that make sense.

Taking the appropriate time to do this thoroughly now will save you editing time later. Don't skimp on this, and don't rush through it by thinking you "already know" what you want to say in any given chapter.

Take time to write it out and check for coherence and completeness. When you've listed all of the chapters with the three points you want to make in each, it'll be easy to see if your reader can follow you through your developmental story and the principles and learnings that you have to teach.

Invest the mental, emotional, and spiritual effort required and spend the time making this flow and feel good. It will keep your energy up and your excitement to get the book done. It will also make writing far easier.

CHAPTER 32

CHAPTER LENGTH

There are lots of ideas about how to write books these days. There are plenty of sources to tell you how long your sentences should be, how long your paragraphs should be, how long your chapters should be, and even how long your book should be.

My experience is it all depends on your topic, your intended audience, and the story you have to tell. My advice, based on writing my own books, reading hundreds of other books, and helping many clients write and market their books, is to write short chapters.

Looking back at literary works of the past, you will find many have tiny print, very dense text, and huge paragraphs as a regular feature. Even my book, *Tightrope of Depression*, has a font that I think is a bit too small. In the next release, I plan to increase the type size to facilitate readability.

Readers today do not read dense blocks of texts, as a rule. Emails with long sentences and complex and lengthy sections get skimmed and not adequately digested. This is a function of how much we are bombarded with an incessant flow of information 24 hours a day, seven days a week.

Current research shows if something is not digestible and actionable in a very short period, we simply gloss over it or put it in the "I'll get back to that later" pile.

You have one of those piles too, and you rarely, if ever, get back in to see what you set aside. You don't want your book to be one of those things.

Go to the bookstore and find books you like. How do they look? How do you want your book to feel when your reader opens it for the first time? That is a great starting point. The second thing to look for is a layout, type size, and paragraph length that attracts you.

In other words, the person you are writing to has many things in common with you. A safe place to start is what you like to read. How big do you want the font? How long do you want the sentences? What kind of vocabulary do you find easy to digest? How long do you want your paragraphs to be?

People often spend just a few minutes at a time reading. You want to structure your book so your reader, in that few minutes, can complete a chapter or even two.

There are certainly notable exceptions to this rule, but I would recommend you write short chapters—two to four pages at most. Your readers will thank you, and the understanding and implementation of what you teach will increase.

Earlier, I said if you want to make more than three points in a chapter, consider splitting it. That is not a "rule," but it increases digestibility. It also helps you write shorter chapters. For example, this book has about 600 to 800 words per chapter.

There are a couple of chapters that are a bit longer because it didn't make sense to split them. You might find that as well. How you do this is obviously your choice, but I promise to give you my best advice and tell you what's working now.

Another example of this idea is the story of the cab ride at the beginning of the book. I could have written it in one long chapter. Instead, I broke it up into three parts. One reason was to keep the chapters short.

There were other storytelling reasons as well, but the chapter-length played a significant role. Write two to four-page chapters. One or two-sentence paragraphs. Use language that is read and understood by a sixth-grade student.

As your reader digests this, you want them focused on the feelings and experiences and not wondering what certain words mean and feeling like they need to have a dictionary nearby.

CHAPTER 33

THREE MEMORY WORDS

After you have all your chapters and feel like you have told the story of your development effectively and presented what you have to teach in a seamless flow, it's time to think about the mechanics of writing.

Something you hear often is, "I have writer's block." Another way this is said is, "I open the computer, get up a blank page, stare at it, and have exactly nothing to say."

There are lots of ways to prevent this from happening and to get past it if it does. This chapter is devoted to one of those techniques.

This is the final step to prepare for the actual writing process. The technique in this chapter will make writing flow smoothly and help you stay in the flow you created.

Get one blank page for each part of the book. Write the names of the chapters in the left-hand column going from top to bottom.

Key Ideas and Memory Words

Key Words	Memory Words
I broke my leg	
• Bad things happen	Friend, trick, pain
• I missed stuff	Tournament, embarrassed, celebrity
• Things heal	Doctor, candy, girls
My parents got divorced	
• Did I cause this?	Fights, trouble, money
• My life is ruined	Scared, teacher, friends
• There is a way	Uncle, team, football
I got accepted	
• Look on the bright side	Angry at teacher, smiling, play anyway
• Have a back-up plan	Grocery store, friends, business, local school
• Never give up	Calling & calling, go visit, laughter

Underneath each chapter title, write the three points you are making in that chapter (see chapter 31). Then for each of the main ideas in a chapter, choose three memory words or short memory phrases. These basically act as a reminder for you.

For example, let's assume I'm writing a book on *How to Create Time*. It is a workshop I teach, and I may write that book someday.

Let's further assume that one of the chapters is about how to use a calendar effectively. The chapter title is "Make Your Calendar Magic."

The three key points for that chapter title would be:

- Calendars – Freedom or Slavery?

- What Goes on the Calendar?

- Flexibility is Power

For the memory words, I would do this:

- Calendars – Freedom or Slavery?

o Mental Hard Drive, Creativity, Joy

- What Goes on the Calendar?

o Truth or Consequences, Colors, Busy/Free

- Flexibility is Power

o Blocks Move, Honesty, Choices

The purpose of the memory words/phrases is so I can freely write about the principle without getting lost. The three phrases under one

---

principle might not mean anything to anyone else. To me, they are very significant.

For example, when I discuss how to use a calendar, one principle is to put everything in it. This increases visibility, allows you to track where your time goes, and helps you make choices about what you mean to do and not do.

It helps you prioritize and say no when your time is already obligated. I would remember all that from the small memory phrase, "Truth or Consequences."

The second memory word, "Colors," is a way to stay balanced in life. If you color everything the same, you can't tell if you're leaving important things out.

For example, if you color all your family activities blue, all your business activities green, all your personal preparation activities orange and all your private time red, you can tell at a glance what your week looks like and if you are neglecting some significant area of life.

To someone else, "Colors" means very little. They might guess, but it would not be a trigger for them like it is for me as I think about what I'm trying to teach.

The third phrase, "Busy/Free," is a tool to help balance my business and personal goals. If I am writing for a large block of a day, I can tell the calendar to view it as "Free" even though it appears busy.

This allows people who have my schedule link to schedule during that time for interviews and prospect calls for my coaching business. Otherwise, the commitment to write would only be in my mind and less likely to happen.

Those very brief explanations are a small part of what I teach about in "What Goes on the Calendar." The phrases are enough to remind me and let me relax as I think about that part of the topic. There's no writer's block because the phrases jog my memory.

The calendar topic is a perfect example. There are several other points that I make when I teach how to use a calendar more effectively to create time. Perhaps, I would have six points that I want to cover instead of three.

Because there are so many, I would probably split using calendars into two chapters. The first chapter would be "Make your Calendar Magic Part I," and the second chapter would be "Make your Calendar Magic Part II.

I would split the topic both for readability, and so a person reading would not have so many things to remember at once. There is a sequential and logical order to the presentation spread over two chapters, just like there will be with your curriculum.

This example illustrates how to create "Three Memory Words," and explains more fully the material in chapter 32, about splitting chapters to keep things digestible.

CHAPTER 34

3 X 5 CARDS AND DICTATION

We are almost ready to start writing. Now you have all of the chapters with titles laid out in a good flow, and you have the three key points for each chapter plus the three memory words/phrases for each. One final preparation step, and you are ready.

This step serves two purposes. First, it's one final trip through your sequence to make sure your ideas are in order. Second, it will be an easy way to write quickly and completely.

Take the three sheets you just wrote and transfer each chapter to a 3 x 5 card. Across the top of the 3 x 5 card, write the chapter title. Then underneath the chapter title, write the three main ideas.

Underneath each idea, write the three memory words. That way you have a 3 x 5 card for each chapter that looks about like this:

3x5 Cards

Chapter: I Broke My Leg

1. Bad things happen
   - Friend
   - Trick
   - Pain

2. I missed stuff
   - Celebrity
   - Embarrassed
   - Tournament

3. Things heal
   - Girls
   - Candy
   - Doctor

Up to this point, we have only talked about the first two sections of the book. What you have prepared now is 3 x 5 cards for the first 2/3 of your book.

Don't worry, the third section of this book will give you instructions about how to create the final section of your book. It won't be hard. Practicing with what you have will make it easy for you to create those 3 x 5 cards, and it will be a snap.

Think about a time that you did a presentation at work or a speech for an audience. Perhaps you had a set of PowerPoint slides.

If you prepare the slides well, there were few words on each slide. No one likes to watch a speaker read the slides. Let's assume you know this and prepared accordingly.

The headers on the PowerPoint slides serve as your topic guides, and the bullet points serve as your memory words. You can give the entire PowerPoint presentation with a clicker in your hand and the slides serving as your guide.

Your stack of 3 x 5 cards functions in much the same way. This is a wonderful way to prepare to write your book in the fastest and easiest way possible.

When your stack of 3 x 5 cards is complete, you can do an additional preparation exercise to see if your book is really ready to go. We will discuss that in the next chapter.

At this point, review the diagram above and go over your developmental story matrix and the framework you have developed to teach your ideas. If it feels good, you are on fire.

The second topic for this chapter is the use of a dictation tool. I use Dragon software by Nuance, but there are other dictation software choices.

The reason I recommend dictation is simple. When you have the 3 x 5 cards in front of you with the three key points for each chapter and the three memory words written under each key point, it's easy to talk your way through the book.

Picture this: pretend you are giving a talk on your topic. If your 3 x 5 cards well prepared, you could speak your entire book to a willing audience.

When we type, unless you are an incredible touch typist, you will look away from the cards and at the keyboard and/or the screen. That will be distracting, and you will regularly lose your train of thought.

Looking at the screen is particularly problematic for two reasons. First, even though voice recognition software is really good, it still makes some mistakes. You will see those and want to fix them.

Second, as you see the words, you will get caught up in analysis and criticism of your thought flow. You will want to edit and make it better.

Both will interrupt your flow and make it take much longer to get your first draft on paper. Dictating let's you look only at the cards and get lost in your own story.

If you choose to type, then look only at the cards, or your keyboard and do not worry about typing mistakes or editing. I have written books, both typing and using dictation. After you get used to the dictating software, which doesn't take long, it is magic.

It allows you to simply look at your cards, stay focused on the story, and speak your truth.

CHAPTER 35

DOES IT FLOW, DOES IT TEACH?

Creating the book is incredibly exciting. There is nothing quite like the sense of accomplishment when you have organized your thoughts, and you are getting ready to present them to the public.

An optional final check before you start is to go through your stack of 3 x 5 cards a few times as if you were speaking to an audience. As you do, answer the two questions posed in the title of this chapter.

Does it flow? In other words, as you slowly turn the cards over one at a time and speak the points you want to make using the memory words as a reminder, does the story make sense and flow in a logical fashion?

If you find yourself stammering, confused, or wondering how to talk about something, then stop and get that fixed. It saves time and frustration later.

So-called "writer's block" happens when we forget what we have to say, get confused about where we are in the story, or can't figure out how to say what we mean. You will reduce your chances of that by going through the cards until it feels like it's easy.

Don't rush this; think about what you'll say and how you will express the three key points for each chapter. Also, check the flow between chapters. As you finish each chapter, does the beginning of the next chapter seem logical, and is it easy to see how one chapter flows to the next?

This is the same process you would do if you were giving a speech. You would go through your cue cards and see if it flowed so that you would not stumble or get stuck standing at the podium.

The second of the two questions, "Does it Teach?" applies to part two of the book. After you have told the story you want to tell, and you teach me what you have learned to help me have a better life, does it work?

Can you go through the 3 x 5 cards explaining the framework, the principles, and the learnings that you have in a fluid and coherent way?

If you get stuck, fix it. Getting stuck in practice runs, means you will definitely get stuck when you're dictating because something about dictating feels a little more "on stage," even though you're only talking to a machine.

After you feel like it flows and it teaches, we're ready to go.

If you're reading this book for the first time, at this point, you will have 3 x 5 cards for the first two-thirds of the book in your hand. Finish part three of this book to create the third section of your own book before you start dictating.

CHAPTER 36

DICTATE

I title this chapter "Dictate," because that is how I write books. If you have decided to type the manuscript, then the name of this chapter should be "Write."

This may seem obvious, and you might wonder why I'm having a chapter on the act of writing. This is not a writing course, and I'm not teaching you how to write. If you want help with that, consult my other works, or get another writing course.

I am going to help you get your book done. An important note here is about creating time to get the work done. One of the biggest things that keep people from finishing their books is discouragement.

Someone decides to write a book; they create a great "outline," and maybe they even start writing. Or, they read or heard somewhere that they should blog regularly and then turn it into a book.

They get started, and it's all exciting. You roll along for a while, and you have an outline and some writing, or maybe you have 50 blog posts.

Then somehow, you get stuck, you lose motivation, something intervenes, you slow down, and then the entire project sits on the shelf and never gets finished.

This chapter is about avoiding that problem. With your story arc finished and the practicing done from the last chapter, it will be clear to you what to write.

The barrier is planning. Most people do not set aside time to write. Here's a way to experiment, figure out how long you need and then calendar the time to get it done.

Take the Story Arc™ and begin dictating (or writing.) Don't fix anything, just write until you have five or six chapters done in the first draft.

Look and see how many words you've written. Microsoft Word has a word count indicator at the bottom of the frame. Most word processing software has a similar feature. Take the word count and divide it by the number of chapters you have.

Now you have an idea of an average chapter length. Let's say it's 600 words. Multiply that by the total number of chapters in your story arc, and you will get an idea of how long your book will be.

As part of the nine questions, you estimated a book-length. Just for reference, compare the two numbers.

You also know how long it took to simply blow through a few chapters without stopping or thinking about editing or anything else. This will be easy to do because you rehearsed it, and it felt good.

If you divide the time it took but the number of chapters you wrote, you will see how long you need to write a chapter.

Let's say it's 30 minutes. If you have 50 chapters outlined in your story arc, you need 25 hours to get a first draft done. The completion of the Story Arc™ lets you write quickly and without delay.

Now go to your calendar and block out 25 hours. I wouldn't recommend working longer than two hours at a stretch. In *The*

Results Equation™, I described how to use timers to work more efficiently. Information on that book is in the appendix.

If you need 25 hours, then that would be 13 two-hour blocks. Put 13 two-hour blocks in your calendar. If you can only work two hours a week, that means it will take 13 weeks to write your first draft.

Thirteen weeks is about 90 days, or three months – which isn't very long. If you have your first draft done in 90 days, you will be miles and miles ahead of those who plan to write a book, and at the end of each year, lament that nothing has happened.

The point of this chapter is just to get going. Start, make some estimates about how long you need based on your first few chapters, put it in your calendar, and then keep moving.

Whether you use dictation software or type a manuscript, it doesn't matter. Use the same method you used for your estimate and put it in your calendar. Let's get that book done.

CHAPTER 37

WRITE, DON'T EDIT

Besides scheduling, there is one other thing that is a significant impediment that slows down every person I have helped write a book.

If you're a new author, you're probably worried about people liking what you write. You also worry about whether you said what you meant.

When you are writing your first draft, just write. If you take the time to stop and edit, you will never finish. There are several reasons for this.

First, it's discouraging. It's difficult to decide the "best" way to say something. You write a paragraph and then rewrite it. Then you decided it should be in a different place. And so it goes.

Maybe you get bold enough to finish an entire chapter. Then those 600 words (if that's how many there are), become a monster around your neck. Working on them until they're just right becomes an obsession.

That becomes so difficult that the idea of writing the next chapter is daunting beyond belief. So you don't. It does downhill from there. Don't do it that way. There will be plenty of opportunities to edit later.

You created a story arc. You created three points to cover in each chapter, and you have memory words to help you with your flow.

You have practiced going through your 3 x 5 cards, and it feels good to you. That means you're ready to write.

So, dictate or write without stopping. If you write for an hour, do not go back and edit – just let the work stand as is.

I have tried many ways to do this, and I find going all the way through the first draft is the way to get the story told and to make sure your project gets finished.

Between the "inner critic," the desire to "do everything right" and a bit of worry about what others might think, it's easy to see why editing at the same time as writing is problematic.

On top of that, when you write, and when you edit, you use different parts of the brain. The writing part of the brain is the right side – the creative, the flowing, the storyteller. This is especially true if you are telling your own story.

Editing uses the left side of the brain. Punctuation, sentence structure, passive versus active verb voice. Structural issues and completeness. All those technical things are handled better in the left brain. In addition, the critical analysis of the story is a more left-brain activity.

If you write and edit at the same time, you keep switching back-and-forth between the right brain and the left brain. When we do this, it incurs a significant "task-switching penalty."

In computer science, that is the cost to the CPU of switching from one application to another. The task switching penalty can be measured in computers. It is also real and significant in your mind.

Between the task switching penalty and the discouragement caused by never quite being satisfied with the way you wrote something, you can spend all day writing a chapter and still not be happy.

The next day, the idea of doing it all over again is not very interesting.

When I wrote earlier about measuring how fast you write, the process I described only works if you don't stop to edit. For example, I can write about 1500 words per hour if I have my story arc done well, my 3 x 5 cards organized, and have practiced.

When I did it the other way, editing and writing at the same time, the pace slows to 200 or 300 words per hour, if that. That is a discouraging process. If you do that, the time you blocked in your calendar won't be anywhere near enough, and the whole exercise will be frustrating.

The editing process is done separately after your first draft is complete. If you want some more information on editing, I have included an appendix at the end of the book describing one approach.

Every publisher has its own editing framework and process, so my appendix is just one way to do it. The point of this chapter is to help you understand you will never get to that stage if you don't just write the draft without worrying about editing in the process.

PART III

CREATING IMPACT

This part of the book covers two topics. First, we will finish the story arc for the third section of your book. The principles you have learned so far will be applied to complete your third section.

When you write a book to serve others, then there are three hurdles you jump to be effective. Each part of the book is designed to address one hurdle. First, in part one, you create a connection with someone. This happens when they recognize events from your life in theirs, and they believe you understand their situation.

Second, in part two, they come to accept that what you teach might help them. They must believe your learning *might* be relevant and true. Your reader becomes certain you have answers – for someone that maybe looks a lot like them.

Every person believes they are unique and special. Everyone, deep in their heart, believes no one understands them completely. Getting over the second hurdle handles that problem.

The third hurdle is the question, "Will this work for me?" Part three of your book is designed to answer this question. After the conversation and teaching, a person must come to believe your experience, and your wisdom is relevant and applicable to them specifically.

This barrier falls by giving examples or case studies of the application of your teaching. By using a variety of examples, you demonstrate different types of people have benefited from what you teach. Then, like in the movie, they can believe the ideas you present will work for them.

Second, we will cover how to leverage your book to have a larger impact. Speaking, courses, and other creations let you affect more people in different ways.

If you are writing this book to help others as I suspect you are, then one goal you have is to create the largest possible impact. You want to reach as many people as possible, share what you learned, and help them live better lives.

Perhaps you also have a goal of making a living. Combining helping people, doing something you love, and making a good living is a ticket to a beautiful and happy life.

Such a goal is within your reach. I live that every day of my life. I am thrilled to share everything I know with you. If I can help you beyond this book, there is contact information in the appendix.

What does it mean to make an impact?

Nearly everyone I help wants to "help people." As we dig into the meaning of that phrase, it usually means using the experience and learning you have to help others avoid pitfalls and have better success than you had.

All over the Internet, there are thousands of people selling the idea you can "teach what you know, help people, and make a living." Let's assume for a moment that this is true if done properly. You have spent a lifetime accumulating wisdom and experience. Presented well and applied to the right people, it can be valuable.

Creating an impact is the process of figuring out how to make that happen. Writing a book is just the beginning. If you write a book and leave it on Amazon or some other digital platform with no other effort, then nothing will happen.

95% of authors don't make much money on their books. Besides, reading a book alone will have a limited impact. How many books have you read that have changed your life just because you read the book?

More likely, real transformation comes from reading a book, hearing a talk or watching a video, and then making choices about what to do so it changes your life. Hopefully, you get a coach to help you clarify exactly what you want, create an action plan, and then help you with suggestions, loving encouragement, and accountability to move forward with your plan.

Creating an impact can be done in multiple ways. One-to-one coaching is one way, creating products and services online of off-line is another way. Teaching workshops is another opportunity, as is speaking engagements.

With the reach of the Internet, expanding faster and faster, virtual lectures, workshops, and teaching is available and far more accessible than doing things in person.

Picking a platform, creating a plan, and following through with regular execution will be the key to creating any kind of impact. My book *The Results Equation*™ was written as a guide to help you create goals and make them your reality.

If you want additional help, there are books listed in the appendix. My contact information is also available in case I can help you on your journey. Above all, your determination to follow through is the key ingredient.

The best of intentions won't matter without grit and follow-through. The first measure of your follow-through is completing a book. Strap in, make a real commitment to yourself, and let's get this finished for your sake and for the sake of those you might help.

CHAPTER 38

THREE QUESTIONS

In the introduction to this section, I talked about three hurdles that people must overcome for your teaching to be effective.

First is creating rapport, which is connecting with them in such a way there is a commonality or bond of some kind.

Second is powerfully sharing your teaching. This will depend on creating a clear and effective framework and then teaching it in a fashion that they can both understand and use.

Third is believing it will work for them. Every one of us has looked at someone successful and said, "sure, it works for them, but not for me."

In the prologue, I told the story of my feeling sitting in an audience of a great speaker. I was convinced while all this wonderful goodness I was hearing could work for someone, I was excluded.

Another way to think about these three hurdles is to ask three questions:

- Do they know you?

- Do they trust you?

- Do they believe you?

These three questions match exactly to the three challenges. In Internet marketing and indeed marketing of all kinds, people talk about "know, like, and trust. That encapsulates the same challenges.

I'm using slightly different language, but the focus is the same. Getting to know you will happen through an artful telling of your developmental story.

Trusting you flows from feeling like you are similar in many ways, and they can see the direct application of the framework you created and the teachings you give.

Believing you is not just believing you're telling the truth. If they don't believe you're telling the truth, they won't trust you, and the framework you present will be useless.

Coming to believe you in the context of this book means they have crossed the threshold of resistance that says that your words won't work for them.

If I had crossed that threshold in the story in the prologue, then I would not have been in tears and anger saying, "Me, I got nothing."

I would've had hope, and a fire kindled in my heart that sounded like "maybe, just maybe I found what I'm looking for. This might be my path to success.

CHAPTER 39

DO THEY KNOW YOU?

In a book, you are delivering a monologue to the reader. You are walking with them through a series of events and circumstances that shaped your life.

You pick the events and tell the stories in a way you hope provides a real insight into who you are, what happened to you, and what you have written about: no games, no exaggeration, just truth.

This can seem like a terrifying task to start with. It can be difficult to share things past the superficial level where most interactions happen. We all share the fear of inadequacy and the yearning to matter.

Helping your reader get to know you is fun, frightening, and essential if you're going to write a book to help people change their lives.

The first five books I wrote were on meditation. Writing those books was easy because meditation was something I knew how to do and something I knew would be useful to people. There wasn't much self-disclosure, and for the most part, I was simply functioning as a teacher.

When I wrote *Tightrope of Depression*, I was terrified. I lost sleep for weeks before the book was published. I was being vulnerable and sharing things from deep in my life I thought might destroy me.

The meditation series has been moderately successful and does help people learn to meditate. It also explores the benefits of meditation in the areas of healing and wellness, learning, spirituality, and personal accomplishment.

Tightrope of Depression has been wildly successful. It has connected me deeply with many people, affected others deeply, and made significant money for my business.

There is no doubt in my mind the level of success directly equates to the level of disclosure and vulnerability—openness and sharing your heart trumps every time.

As you think about your reader "getting to know you," it doesn't mean you are writing a "tell-all" book. There will be a level of appropriate disclosure. There will be things you do not want to talk about, and there will be other things that don't make sense to share in the context of the book you're writing.

But if you want your book to have a significant impact, you need to be open. Write it from your own experience and truth and with the intent to help your readers with difficult challenges.

As I help various clients write books, their willingness to tell the truth and be open is one of the biggest areas of work. How much to tell, how to talk about difficult things, and how to frame the learnings productively and powerfully.

Carefully working through this as you create your story arc, the flow of your chapters, and the things you will teach in the framework takes significant effort. Putting in that work is a big predictor of success.

Another element here is how you plan to leverage the book. Is it going to be an element of your social media strategy? Are you going to create a course or courses that come from your framework?

Is what you write about in your book consistent with the image that you present on social media? If there is a disconnect, your readers will not feel they know you because they don't really know which one is the real you.

All these things have a direct bearing on how well your book will succeed. It all comes directly from how well the reader connects with you in the book.

CHAPTER 40

DO THEY TRUST YOU?

It's easy to write a book and tell people what they should do. Maybe you know what you're talking about, and maybe you don't. How will the reader know?

A tragic but real example will illustrate. I had a family doctor who was overweight, obviously did not care for themselves in a meaningful way, and appeared just to be going through the motions.

It was easy to go to the doctor's office, make complaints about whatever medical issues were bothering me, and get prescriptions I wanted for symptom remediation.

How much trust do you think was in that relationship? I doubt the doctor knew anything about me in a significant way. I had no confidence that their analysis and prescriptions were well thought out.

I did significant research online ahead of time and came to the doctor with a plan. I proposed my own diagnosis of the problem and suggested the solution. As long as my "diagnosis" was not outrageous, and what I requested was not silly, I got what I wanted.

As a former drug addict, I was careful not to ask for anything I thought would be risky to me in any way. But I certainly could have taken advantage of the situation. In that circumstance, there was no trust in the relationship whatsoever.

I made my own diagnosis and used the doctor as a portal to access pharmaceuticals and referrals to other specialists. It worked for what I needed, but it would not be a good way to treat a potential beneficiary of your book.

Part one of your book talks about your development. When you move from your own life experience into part two, where you teach what you learned, you are essentially offering something a lot like a prescription.

The reader connects with you in part one by identifying with some of your stories and situations. Then they get your framework and solutions in as a "prescription" in part two. But remember, this is still a monologue.

If you do a good job in part one, the reader will be receptive in part two. They will approach your framework and teaching with an open mind and an expectation of success.

Your goal here is to affect change, not just to inform. In the context of this monologue, you need to present your framework and your suggested ideas and actions in a clear and accessible way that feels believable and useful.

In other words, for the framework to make any difference in the life of the reader, they must trust you. If you build The Story Arc™ as I have explained it, your framework and teaching will feel truthful and convincing.

This will maximize the opportunity and the likelihood the reader will connect with your framework and at least consider suggestions and solutions you propose.

Remember, trust is a delicate thing. Write with a single reader in mind – that specific person you pictured at the beginning. That will be the best way to be simple, clear, and persuasive.

CHAPTER 41

DO THEY BELIEVE YOU?

This question may feel a lot like the previous chapter, but it is far more profound. In this context, believing is one step beyond trust. The reader may trust you're telling the truth. The reader may trust the things you describe in your framework working for you and may work for somebody else.

The question of belief here applies to them individually. In the final analysis, the reader must believe you enough to think what you have said could work for *them*.

So how do we go about making that happen?

As the author of a book, you have a certain level of prestige. Most people could not imagine themselves writing a book or seeing themselves listed on Amazon as an author.

Because of this, it is easy for someone to read your book and say, "well, that might be true for you, but I'm different. I can't do that."

It's fun for us to read books about real people who acted in powerful ways or about legends and superheroes. We read those books and don't believe we could be that person.

The challenge in getting someone to believe you is to get past the sense that "while your story is interesting and your advice might be good, it's not right for me."

We have to identify with them well enough and feel "real enough" to them, so they begin to believe what you teach is accessible to them, even though they don't have prestige as an author or "measure up" in some other way.

One way to do that is to give examples of your framework in action. If they can see examples where other people used what you teach, and it works, it's a start. Your advice must apply to regular people and people just like them. If they see that, they have a higher level of confidence that your solution might be what they need.

You can make all the fantastic claims and promises you want, but until the reader can identify strongly enough with you and with the examples you teach, they won't believe "this will work for me."

The Story Arc™ in the third part of the book is a journey guiding your reader through possibilities where they can see themselves in the stories you tell.

Finishing part two of the book means you completed your teaching. You laid out your framework with all of its principles and applications.

In part three, each chapter will be a story. A real story about a real person you helped. The purpose of the stories is to use the framework you have just taught to show transformation and success.

One of the most powerful principles in writing and speaking is "show, don't tell." By giving real examples with specifics about struggle, transformation, and eventual victory, you create the possibility your reader will believe you.

When you create the Story Arc™ for part three, start with the same blank spreadsheet you used for part one. If you can, pick examples of people you helped. You can also use examples of people you know who used the principles in your framework and had success.

Fill out the spreadsheet just like you did for part one. Column one is the name of the person or a name you create for the situation.

Column two is a description of the problem before the transformation was attempted. Column three is a description of how your framework was applied—which principles, how long it took, and the path through the problem to success.

Column four is a description of the outcome after work and transformation. Completing this spreadsheet will take a few iterations as you decide what the right level of disclosure is and how to tell the story effectively.

To tell your developmental story in part one, you needed ten to twenty events that shaped your life. In part three, you only need four or five good examples of how your framework was applied.

Make the examples as different as possible. Don't tell the same story five times. Use people with different problems from different walks of life, using different parts of the framework or, if possible, all the framework.

This may seem difficult right now as you think about it. To make it easier, the next few chapters will give you some examples of stories you can use to create the chapters for part three.

CHAPTER 42

YOUR STORY OF SUCCESS

The first and most obvious example should be your own story of success. In part one of the book, you gave different events through your life that were the foundation of your ability to create the framework you present in part two.

In part two of the book, there will be simple examples of how you and perhaps others used one or more of the principles taught successfully.

Neither of these is a complete description of your own transformation. Devoting a chapter to describe yourself before you applied your framework and following your life through the changes that made you better and brought you to a happier place will be a compelling and very relatable story.

The chapter about your transformation will take a little effort because the changes in your own life probably took place over a long period. Presumably, you discovered these principles haphazardly and applied them one at a time.

Describing the journey from a macro level about who you were, how you've changed, and who you are now is a validation of your own success and demonstration of how the principles and framework affected your life in positive ways.

This is not about bragging or making yourself a hero. In fact, this may be the least heroic of the stories in part three. Because you took months and perhaps years or even decades to transform yourself, it will not seem heroic at all.

Using a good editor will be key here. As noted, this chapter is not about making you the hero. It's about showing what you teach works. You are a different and happier person today because you learned and applied the principles taught in part two.

In *Tightrope of Depression*, my transformation took decades. I put a summary of things I do now to stay healthy and master depression at the end of part three.

It's not necessary to put your story first or last. Decide where it fits best based on how it relates to the principles you teach, the framework you have, and the other stories you will include.

There isn't a perfect way to write this story. There is no perfect placement. Get some help with this story. In the appendix on editing, you will get ideas about how to use an editor effectively for both this piece and for the rest of the book.

CHAPTER 43
CASE STUDIES PART I

A typical way to refer to success stories about the application of any system or process is to call them "case studies." A case study is simply an example of an outcome using a method or system with a particular person or company.

The first type of case study would be people you have worked with. I'm a coach, so for me, that would be coaching clients. If you are a therapist, that might be patients.

If you are a physical trainer, that will be the clients trained. If you work with trauma healing, that will be people you helped heal through your processes.

If you help families with small children, it will be examples of families you worked with. Anyone you had as a client in a professional capacity easily qualifies as a "case study."

There is another group of people who also qualify as "case studies."

You may not yet have a business helping people using things you teach. This is the case with coaches just starting, and it's also the case with people who do volunteer work or work in various positions in corporations.

As a director in a corporate situation, I had a manager who was having serious self-doubt issues after he got a promotion and had to run a department. I "coached" that manager in several one-to-one meetings over a few months. We did not call it "coaching," I was simply doing my job.

Later, that manager was promoted to a director position and won a prestigious "Director of the Year" award two years after that. The recognition he received was specifically for his excellence in managing people. This skill was precisely what we had been working on in our "coaching" sessions.

That is an excellent case study, although the setup was such that I might have missed it when looking for proof my framework and principles were effective.

Whether you have an established business or not, some of your most effective case studies will be individuals you have worked within non-traditional situations.

Some examples include:

- Community volunteer work

- Church volunteer work

- Boy Scouts or Girl Scouts

- Family situations

- Community sports organizations

- Friends who confide in you

- Many other situations

The point is simple. Your life experience made you the right person for whatever was happening. You took advantage of things you knew and offered assistance in solving a problem or bettering a difficult situation.

If it's clear you can point to one or more of the principles or parts of the framework you create in part two, these are case studies about the effectiveness of your teaching.

Undoubtedly, your ability to create success came directly from your own learning as your life had been shaped by the stories of part one.

If you look at your life, you will find many case studies that aren't "business-related," but are very appropriate for demonstrating the effectiveness of your framework. Use them.

Chapter 44

Case Studies Part II

The obvious case studies to use are those that come from your clients. If you have a business doing all or part of the work taught in your framework, then successes in any of these situations will be effective case studies for part three.

In selecting these case studies, confidentiality is important, and you should always simply refer to someone as "a client."

You can refer to "case studies" when talking about those who did not pay you as well. The fact that they didn't pay you has nothing to do with it. If you simply use "client" as the designation in every situation, then anonymity will be even further protected.

As you think about case studies for part three, here are some guidelines that will help you pick those that are most effective in helping your reader believe you.

1. Choose as many different kinds as you can. Different ages, different income levels, different problems, different uses of the same parts of the framework, different lengths of time it took to work through the problem.

The point here is to give your reader as many opportunities as possible to see themselves in the context of the situations you are sharing.

2. Remember the example of movies. Actors and actresses never look into the camera. They never "break the fourth wall." Yet all the

moviegoers have no problem seeing themselves in the characters, in the situations and in the emotional web woven by the film.

Similarly, a reader who is genuinely looking to solve a problem will be able to see themselves in various aspects of the case studies you present. That will more effectively allow them to believe you and want to apply the framework you teach to their own problems.

3. The framework for telling case studies is very simple.

a. Start with the "before" situation. What was going on that drives the need to make a change?

b. Describe the process. Did you have regular meetings (as I did with the individual I supervised,) was there written correspondence, videos that were shared, etc.

c. How did you and the person in the case study interact? How often, how long? For example, you could say, "my client and I met weekly for about an hour over three months. "In that time, she learned the principle of (whatever your teaching). She was gradually able to make changes in the way she handled the problem she started with. After three months, it was no longer an issue, and she felt like it was completely solved."

That's just one way to tell the story, and it illustrates all the components used in helping someone understand how it all worked. You will want to experiment and see what works best for your framework and teaching.

4. When talking about the principle(s) applied, provide as much detail as is appropriate for the part or parts of the framework in

action. Give plenty of specifics so your reader can feel the effects and have more opportunity to see it working for them.

CHAPTER 45

CASE STUDIES PART III

Sometimes it's appropriate to use a person as a case study you never worked with, either in a volunteer capacity or in a paid professional capacity. These case studies are a bit different, but they can help you establish credibility and evidence.

Celebrities, community icons and others are regularly in the public eye. Their lives are open to celebration and criticism. Often what they do is public knowledge or is already shared in magazines or books. Sometimes these can be effective case studies.

It is not uncommon to read about spectacular failure or amazing transformation that happened to some well-known person. Often, much is shared about how they did that work.

If it's clear from reading or watching the available information about that person and the change that took place, some things in your framework or principles were involved, it is completely appropriate to refer to that as a case study.

Don't make any false claims about your involvement. Your point here is simply to show already known, and high-profile situations, something in your framework was used effectively and powerfully to create the kind of transformation your reader might want.

In fact, a person reading that may wonder how to do the very same work the celebrity did. Your framework may be their ticket to accessing the success and power of that principle.

The idea here is not to do "name dropping." The idea is to help your reader see various ways all or part of the framework you teach have been used successfully to make changes and improvements exactly like they seek.

In describing such public case studies, stick to what is known or revealed in other books, interviews, television programs, and other public material.

Case studies of this type can be very effective in persuading someone to get off the starting block and move into the lane of progress.

CHAPTER 46

MY BOOKS

This book is written to help you write your book. When I first started writing books, I did not have *The Story Arc*™ as a guide for how to organize my material and write my books.

Consequently, the first books I wrote (a five-part series on meditation) were more difficult than the last six books I have written.

I struggled to organize an outline. I didn't know what to put first. I wasn't sure what would be the best flow through the book. I slaved for weeks over an outline and an order in which to present the material.

Finally, I realized I wanted to take my reader on a logical journey from one end of the book to the other. To do that, I had to know where the journey started. That meant I had to make some assumptions about the reader.

I had to assume they were interested in the topic. I had to assume they had at least a passing knowledge of meditation. Or did I?

All these questions were swirling around, and as I thought through all this, I started making notes about this journey my reader would take.

Gradually I built the Story Arc™. Suddenly organizing and then writing books became easy. By being clear with myself about what I thought the reader might or might not already know, I was able to include instructions about chapters they could skip or others they could emphasize depending on their existing knowledge.

That gave me confidence, the reader would be able to follow the story and teaching no matter what their skill level or previous experience.

It was like magic, and it made every book from then on fun to organize and a joy to write. I was no longer worried about anything in the process.

Using the Story Arc™ as outlined, I have written a book in three weeks. I have helped other clients do the same thing. The key is not in the writing. The key is the organizational work that takes place before the writing begins. The homework upfront is the magic.

Tightrope of Depression has turned out to be the first book of the trilogy. I certainly never imagined that would happen. Using the Story Arc™ process, I was able to take the first book, imagine what a longer journey would look like, and then make a "trilogy arc" through the second and third volumes.

When I wrote Tightrope, I had no intention of writing more than one book. I was writing my story, and that was the end of it. It was only after that book was complete and a couple of years went by I realized my story of depression, living as a creative with depression was just starting.

I had so much to do and to say. I knew I had so much to offer. I knew that my thoughts about how to both manage and overcome this was an ongoing story and was nowhere near finished.

I took the original Story Arc™ and extended it through the years that had passed. This allowed me to see where the reader ended the first journey and where they would pick up the second journey.

By the time I planned the second book, I had realized that there would be a third one, so I completed the arc for both the second and third volumes at the same time.

As I write this book now, volume two of that trilogy, titled *Down from the Gallows*, is due out in fall 2020. Volume three will be finished sometime at the end of 2021 or early 2022.

Having this tool makes it easy to think about more books, more teaching, and more value I can bring into the world. I can't wait to see what you create.

CHAPTER 47

MY CLIENTS

Over the years, I have had several clients who have written books. My primary coaching work is not about writing, but it turns out many who want coaching also realized they have a story to tell.

Here is a sample of people I have helped write books using this process.

- A marketing agency owner who introduced a groundbreaking technique for creating a following.
- A doctor who told her own story of abuse, recovery, and blossoming into a powerful force for helping others.
- An entrepreneur who took a giant risk making a life change, getting out of corporate work, and opening a small business half a world away.
- A coach who decided it was time to tell her own story of addiction and recovery because she found it was helpful in working with her own clients.
- Another coach who told about a traumatic upbringing and how her own work created power for her to do her coaching. She also created a program she now uses to enroll clients.
- A leadership trainer who developed unique ideas and skills to build her own highly successful leadership training and coaching career.

- A financial expert who wanted to take her skill developed through years of financial work and help entrepreneurs building businesses get venture funding.

The list goes on and on. Like I advised you to do in creating success stories, that list is a wide variety of clients from a large pool to give you a sense of different things that have been done and can be done.

For you, the choice is whether you want to go through the effort of organizing your experiences and learning into a framework to help others.

Remember, writing the book is only the beginning. Most authors don't make much money selling books. Most books don't sell tons of copies on Amazon or in bookstores. The key is what follows.

With the ease and unlimited reach of the Internet, your ability to reach potential clients all over the world and have a significant impact is big today and growing bigger every year.

You can have any impact you want in any group and at any level. The question is simply whether you are willing to do the work to make it happen.

CHAPTER 48
WHAT ELSE CAN YOU DO?

A question I get all the time, either before we start the book or as we near the end, is this: "What else can I do?" That question usually means two things.

Often, it is a marketing question. "How can I spread the word about my book and get people to buy it." The other usual interpretation is, "How can I create other things that will help me not only sell the book but spread the message and get people the benefit I intend?"

The things you can do are limited only by your imagination. I will give you some examples of things that I have done, clients have done, I have seen others do, and I have planned for myself soon.

After that, your imagination will be the key.

Here are some marketing things that I have done, my clients have done, or I have seen others do.

- **Book launch parties.** Marketing to get people together to an event either physically or virtually, to celebrate the launch of the book. I have seen such events be simple or complicated, catered, and with entertainment or less formal. Whatever you think will appeal to your audience.
- **Social media book events.** This is an online version of a book launch party, which may include readings, guest speakers, gifts, and perhaps other authors as well.

- **Collaboration events.** Multiple authors who have recently launched books in different but related categories who pool resources and lists to celebrate each other's accomplishments and make their own tribe aware of other's accomplishments.
- **Book reading drip.** The author reads sections of the book, perhaps a chapter at a time, released once or twice a week as an enticement to both buy the book and get involved in the author's circle of influence.
- **Book trailers.** This is like a movie trailer where either the author or some hired talent creates a short trailer dealing with the book. This can be a simple explanation or a full-on dramatization of events or principles taught in the book.
- **Video series.** This is a series of videos that the author does that is much like the book reading except that instead of reading, the videos talk about real-life circumstances related to the book topic.
- **Book launch pages on Pinterest.** Pinterest is a very visual medium, and topically relevant books can do very well in that venue. Issues related to health and beauty, travel, pets, children, jewelry, and fashion, are high-volume topics on Pinterest.
- **Blog series.** A month-long series of blog posts fashioned after the framework taught and the examples given in the book.
- **Copies of books deposited surreptitiously in bookstores.** Going around putting books in bookstores was a strategy used by the authors of the "Chicken Soup" series. They couldn't get a publishing deal, so they went around the country and gave hundreds or perhaps thousands of copies

away by placing them in bookstores. Eventually, they got a deal, and the success has been the stuff of legend.

- **Radio and TV.** Finding topically relevant radio and television programs or podcasts to discuss the book topic and market the book.

These are just a few of dozens, if not hundreds of different ways to market the book and related programs. Many don't cost anything. Social media posting is free and can be effective if done well. Success is solely dependent on the grit and determination to keep going until something big happens.

There are plenty of places to get help. Many businesses make their living advising on how to market books. It is also something I do in my coaching practice and in collaboration with my wife, Joy, who runs a publishing company.

The traditional route of writing a book proposal, finding a literary agent, having the agent pitch the book to untold numbers of publishers, and hoping to get a book advance is, for all intents and purposes, dead. It still happens, but it's rare.

Until you have individually created success and demand for your book and the work you teach, you will not find publishers knocking on your door, check in hand.

CHAPTER 49

KEYNOTES, WORKSHOPS, COURSES, ETC.

Well over 90% of authors make very little money on the book itself. Of most books published, nearly 90% of authors sell fewer than 250 copies of their book. That is not discouraging, it is simply a fact.

When you plan what to do after you write the book, being aware of those facts, and having a plan is the key to success.

In the last chapter, I listed a few ways to promote your book. There are hundreds more and hundreds of companies that will sell you services to get your book in bookstores, hospitals, airports, and everywhere else you can think of.

This chapter will talk about other things besides selling the book that can spread your message, create a buzz around your name and your work, and make you some money.

One such effort is to do some speaking. This may sound daunting, but it can start simply. I know one author who did his first speaking engagement by simply renting a large room at a local restaurant, advertising about the book and the talk locally, and then giving a speech.

Because of the diligent work, there were more than 50 in attendance, a number of books were sold, and a couple of other speaking engagements were secured. You never know who is in the audience when you are speaking. Even if you're talking to a crowd of two people, you are best served if you create the same excitement, the same intensity, and the same purpose you would in an arena of 20,000.

Speaking may not be something you want to do. It might scare you. If you decide it's an appropriate method to spread your message based on your topic, then you will need to get help learning how to speak.

Everyone has heard of Toastmasters, and that is the entry-level point. There are speaking coaches and marketing companies that specialize in getting speaking opportunities.

You will need to create a speaker "one-sheet" and get specific about the things you want to talk about. Record every speech you give, especially during the first year. It will help you get better and help you get more gigs. Event planners want to see a 10-minute clip of you speaking continuously. They are not interested in "sizzle reels."

Workshops are another avenue to both spread the message of the book and gather a tribe. For example, I have taught workshops both online and in-person based on books I've written.

I did a workshop on *How to Create Time* for the staff of a commercial construction company. I did another workshop called *Four Steps to Awesome Client Creation* for a mortgage broker and their sales team.

I did a workshop on finding balance in life when work is extremely busy and hectic for a commercial painting company. This workshop also talked about office efficiency and communication.

I have done online versions of those workshops and several more. Filling the online workshops was done through social media, organic traffic, and word-of-mouth advertising. The key was getting the right help and perseverance.

Business networking groups are everywhere. Learning about the needs of those attending such groups could present you with an opportunity to be a speaker at an event or converse with someone you meet there about the needs their company might have.

Which of these things might be appropriate depends entirely on your topic, who needs to hear you and the preferences you have about what you want to do

Another easy outcome of writing a book is to create an online course. There are tens of thousands of courses online about every topic imaginable. That is not discouraging. Many more are needed.

For example, I got some new software for video editing. I choose the course based on how new it was, even though another site had far more courses in their library.

You may want to create one or two courses and put them in those libraries. You may want to create an online course you teach yourself. Here is a tiny sample of topics taught online.

- Music lessons of all kinds.

- Gardening skills and techniques.

- Project management skills.

- Photography techniques and tools.

- Procrastination accountability groups.

- Goal setting and achievement groups.

- Book writing groups (imagine that).

Every imaginable topic has a dozen courses already in existence. And thousands more come into existence each week. I subscribe to a number of these libraries because I do video editing and work in my recording studio.

The software I use is regularly updated. New recording and mixing techniques are continuously created, and as a professional, I want to stay up to speed.

I have a client who teaches classes both online and in-person about communicating with deceased loved ones and manifestations of the afterlife.

There is no limit to the number of things you could do to increase circulation, raise awareness, and teach the topic about which you have written.

In the chapter on "Getting Help," I will give you some ideas about how to find the right help to get these things done, so you don't waste a lot of time and money in the process.

This shortlist is just a sample and by no means exhaustive. I urge you both to write your book and then be creative about ways you can spread your message, serve your audience, and make a living.

The key is going to be vision, imagination, and hard work. There is no magic wand, and there is no silver bullet. There are good coaches and lots of people with deep experience who will help you.

CHAPTER 50

THE NINE QUESTIONS PART III

I introduced the nine questions in part one, chapter 11. We have discussed all of them except the last two. This chapter is to address those final two questions.

Remember, the nine questions are things you think about before you even start writing the book. Often people ask about publicity and making money after they are in the middle of the book writing process.

As you will see from the answers to these last two questions, the time to start thinking about, planning, and acting on the future is in parallel with the very beginning of the process as you create your developmental story and The Story Arc™.

1. Why are YOU writing THIS book NOW?
2. Who is the book for?
3. When your ideal reader finishes the book, closes the cover and puts it down, what do you want them to do at that moment?
4. What kind of a book is it?
5. What is the voice of the book?
6. How long do you think the book will be?
7. What research will be involved?
8. **After the book is completed, what else are you going to do?**
9. **How are you planning to publish your work?**

Chapters 48 and 49 talked about possibilities related to question number eight. If you are going to have a successful launch not only of the book but of your principles and framework, these answers have to move from the conceptual domain to actual plans.

So far, all we've done is talk about what is possible. Right now, the challenge before you is to decide what you are going to do. What avenues seem most logical to pursue?

When I work with clients to help them write books and then turn those books into opportunities to create business and influence, we consider several things when answering question number eight.

How much time do you plan to spend promoting the book? If you don't have time or staff to find speaking opportunities and look for radio interviews and podcast appearances, that won't be a good choice.

If all you really wanted to do was write the book to get it out there, put it on Amazon and see what happens? Without promotion, the likely answer is nothing will happen.

If you have an aggressive plan, with a desire to have the book and the things you teach have an impact, make a difference to a group of people and make money, you need to pick the venue and plan your strategy.

Here are some questions that will be helpful:

- What is the age group of people you are targeting?
- What is the income of people you are targeting?
- Where do people in your target market go for information?

- How serious is the problem you're solving?
- How hard is it for people to find answers?
- How much competition exists in solving this problem?
- Is the situation or problem increasing or decreasing as time goes on?
- Will technology change the nature or solutions to the problem?
- Is the problem related to a particular generation?
- And several others.

If you choose to make a course to sell online, you need to decide if it's simply a "Do it yourself" or an interactive type course.

Years ago, do-it-yourself courses were popular. Now it is easier to sell a course if there is some interaction and a place to go for help. You must decide how involved you plan to be after you launch your book and follow-up material in the world.

Question nine is partly preference and partly technical. I have seen many people try to publish a book themselves and end up with something that looks like it was done in their kitchen.

There is a difference between "publishing yourself" and "self-publishing." Publishing yourself means that you do the editing, formatting, and the rest of the requirements to get it up online, all yourself.

I've never seen anyone do that well. I have seen a lot of books with wrong-sized margins, difficult-to-read font, pictures off-center, and all the other hallmarks of the do-it-yourself hack job.

Since you've gone to the trouble to write a book, make it look good by getting professional help for the cover, layout, and completing the requirements to put it into the world. You can still "self-publish," which simply means you are the publisher of your own book.

If you want publishing help, there are many small publishers that can help you with all these requirements. Some of them want royalties, but many will not. Getting good advice about how to get your book published is essential.

The last thing you want to do is go through the trouble of pouring out your heart and soul and then putting out an inferior product that looks second-rate and doesn't stand up next to other books on the shelf at your local bookstore.

The appendix contains contact information for a publisher that can give you guidance and information about how to get your work professionally finished.

CHAPTER 51

YOUR PLATFORM

Another key piece of creating success after your book is finished is choosing your platform. A platform is the primary vehicle you use to make your book known to the public and market to your audience.

For example, a platform can be one or more of the social media platforms. You could decide to have an intensive organic campaign on Facebook based on the demographic of your expected reader and the following that you create during the writing and editing portions.

Facebook is enormous and has reach among certain demographics all over the world. Depending on who you're talking to and what you want them to do, that could be useful.

Remember, any platform you choose, owned, or controlled by someone else, can disappear or change the rules at a moment's notice.

The owners of many social media platforms have been accused of suppressing certain kinds of speech because it doesn't line up with their corporate values. Remember, social media platforms are owned by others and do not have legislative or regulatory mandates.

You can ignore social media altogether and decide to use traditional media. Radio shows are looking for content all the time. Depending on your audience, there are radio shows that might be appropriate as a launch platform for your ideas.

In addition to traditional AM and FM radio, there is now Internet radio. It's sometimes difficult to completely distinguish between a podcast and Internet radio, but the difference is significant. An Internet radio show has a regular broadcast schedule and guests, just like a radio show on the airwaves.

YouTube and other video platforms also have shows with episodes and regular broadcasts. Depending on the content and audience of your book, this may be appropriate for you.

Podcasting is the most popular form of communication today. At the time of this writing, podcasts are consumed over any type of media. Podcasts are free, and they are relatively easy to set up.

There are thousands upon thousands of podcast hosts looking for guests to be part of their show. Researching and finding appropriate shows could be an excellent venue.

These are just some of the ideas and places that are available today. In a year or two, the assortment will be different, the audiences will be different and the reach will be different.

The point of this chapter is to encourage you to think intentionally about the platform you want to use and compare it to the audience who uses that platform and the skill and dedication you will bring to making that platform work for you.

Traditional bookstores still exist, but many have gone out of business. Many have diversified and become social gathering places and coffee shops. That trend may continue and could serve you well.

Getting a coach who is knowledgeable about marketing and various platforms will be critical to your distribution success.

Above all, don't just write the book and put it on-line or put it only on your website. That guarantees few sales, little attention and ultimately a disappointing experience considering all the effort you put into the project

CHAPTER 52

YOUR MARKETING

This book is not a marketing manual. There are thousands of books and courses about marketing across all media and venues.

What I want to do here is to encourage you to think about marketing. In the old days, publishers did marketing for authors they published.

Today that is no longer true. Large publishers will ask you about the size of your tribe as part of considering distribution for your book. If you have not created some social media buzz and gathered a significant tribe, you will have difficulty getting the attention of any mid or large tier publisher.

Small publishers will charge you a fee to do the technical work and get the book up on digital platforms, but may not include any marketing. Some publishers offer marketing services, but those are usually extra and negotiated and performed after the book is completed.

Marketing is the process of making your book available to the public and creating awareness in your intended audience both of its existence and content.

Choosing your target tribe and launching intentional and concerted effort to involve them and invite them to participate in your work, and your message will be the central focus of your marketing.

In planning and writing the book, you spent the majority of your time carefully considering the journey your reader would take and then creating the story arc to take them on that journey. That's where the real work is. After your arc is created, your chapters finished, and your message laid out, the writing itself is not difficult.

Marketing is the same way. There are many people who will tell you, "give me a few thousand dollars, and I will market for you." That is a money pit.

Carefully consider your audience, the message, the method you're going to use to reach them, and how to intentionally build the following you want using the platform you choose. Marketing is not a mystery. It is a carefully crafted process. The principles to make it work are well understood.

Your job is to think carefully about who you want to reach and how you want to accomplish this. You also need to consider thoughtfully your willingness to be engaged and stay active as you build a tribe and make the most out of the work you just completed.

Writing a book and "putting it out there," is merely the beginning of the work that you must do in spreading the message from your life experience.

Marketing is a long game. You will need to be in it until you're successful. Just like creating a story arc, your marketing plan will have several parts and will be intended to take both your potential client and your business on a journey from where you are to the pot of gold at the end of the rainbow.

If you want my help with any of the marketing, either with the idea phase or with execution, there is contact information in the appendix.

Whether you use my help or someone else's, make a choice to invest in yourself, your success, and the power of your message by thoughtfully and intentionally pursuing powerful marketing to get your truth into the world.

CHAPTER 53

YOUR SUCCESS

O ften as a coach, I have people who come and want me to "make them a rock star." They somehow view a business coach as a person who can do all the work to get the right people to see how great they are.

I suppose that comes from the day when garage bands went and found a record company that signed them to a contract and then did all the work to get them on stages and in concert halls.

Of course, all those bands got ripped off and ended up poor and not even owning the rights to their own music—a hard lesson to learn.

Regardless of that era, today, your success will depend 100% on you. Your commitment, your dedication, your decision to get help, your choice to stick with it until you see the end of the rainbow – is all on you.

You have a message. You have divine gifts and capabilities. You have a group of people who will benefit from your message. Those things are true.

Whether you create success and help those you could help will depend on your vision, your perseverance, your willingness to create connections, and your determination to see it through to the end.

Some people talk about "being in the right place at the right time." Serendipity is a real thing. It comes to those who put forth all diligence and effort to create success.

One way to say that is "you create your own luck." That's absolutely true. One sad example of the opposite is those who win big lotteries. Over 90% of such people are broke and in trouble within five years.

A cruel joke to be sure, but not surprising because they didn't do the work to create their wealth. Your success will depend on you creating your opportunities and then taking advantage of them.

I teach a class called *Five Essential Skills for Entrepreneurs.* Whether you are an entrepreneur in the other areas of your life or not, you are with respect to moving your book into the world and creating some success.

The five essential skills are:

1. **Take responsibility.** No one is going to do this for you. You might enroll others to help you, and you might have good fortune here and there. But the responsibility for making something happen is yours.

2. **Accept and deal with head trash.** Head trash is that voice inside you that tells you you're not good enough or that you somehow can't make it. Sometimes it's the voice of friends, loved ones, family, and those who should support you. We all have head trash. Accept that fact and create methods to deal with it, so it doesn't stop you from your destiny.

3. **Learn to meditate.** This might seem weird. It's not. It is the most powerful force you do keep your energy up, keep yourself healthy, and create success. If you want help with that, there are references in the appendix.

4. **Love yourself.** This might seem weird also. It's the most important ingredient in the recipe for creating success. Start loving yourself today.

5. **Have fun.** Creating an awesome masterpiece and putting it in the world is the most rewarding and, yes, terrifying thing you can do. If you're not having fun doing it, then you're doing it wrong.

All the success that anyone else has ever had is available to you. There is more opportunity in the world today than there has ever been. Prosperity in much of the world is at an all-time high. The Internet reaches every audience in the world.

Technology is magic and lets you do things today that were inconceivable only a few years ago. Now that you have become one of the 1% who actually writes the book they thought they should write, move into action and go boldly forward.

CHAPTER 54

GETTING HELP

The most terrible myth that exists in our culture today is that somehow asking for help demonstrates weakness. That is false.

Knowing when to ask for help, being willing to go get it, and accepting help are essential in the quest for success. Just ask anyone who has ever achieved significant objectives. No one of any renown has accomplished their life's work without tremendous help from many people.

Today, you have the opportunity to get all the information you want for free, and Google seems to know everything. Finding out how to do anything is possible. That's not the kind of help I'm talking about.

As a coach, my observation is: "It is seldom that we don't know what to do. It is far more often that "we don't do what we know."

Life gets in the way, we get discouraged, head trash makes us doubt our purpose, we "run out of time," and we create excuses for everything.

Honestly, completing big tasks is difficult. If it were easy, everyone would write the book they want to write, everyone would be at the Olympics, and everyone would have the kind of success they want. That's not happening.

This chapter is a plea for you to get the help you need. Hire a coach. Use your coach ruthlessly to deal with your own doubts, head trash, and skill development.

Hire a publisher who can help you get good editing and get a great looking layout and cover. Hire a marketer to help you get your book in the hands of the right people.

Yes, it costs some money. So what? Invest in yourself and your message. Be wise and be one of the smart ones. Get the help you need.

If you want my help with any of the processes we've talked about, contact information is in the appendix. I can't wait to read your masterpiece.

EPILOGUE

The M.C. of the event sat down, and it was my turn to take the stage. I had just been introduced as the single presenter for a conference that lasted an entire day. Subtracting breaks and lunchtime, I had seven hours of the audiences' undivided attention.

At other times in my life, the idea of entertaining, educating, and holding the attention of a group of people for that long would have terrified me. I would've assumed it was impossible, and the entire thing would be a gigantic bust.

Now, I was completely confident and had nothing but success on my mind. I knew for sure I would be able to hold their attention, provide great value, and come away feeling completely satisfied at the end of the day.

I told stories, answered questions, and taught powerful truths that kept the audience riveted and breathless during the entire time.

I sold books, made money, and was asked to come back and speak again. More opportunities came from this event. I was happy.

I had done what I meant to do. The audience was thrilled, the owner of the event was grateful, and I had created another successful experience.

Two things made all the difference:

1. I was teaching from a book I had written called The "Book of Context.

2. I had prepared my presentation using the Story Arc™.

The Book of Context was written to teach something I learned during my near-death experience four months earlier. At that time, I had the extraordinary experience of dying while in a coma and then returning to this world. I had some conversations with God at the door between life and eternity.

During the second of those conversations, some powerful truths had been given, and I had subsequently written them into a book.

I can already hear some readers saying, "Well, if I had an experience like that, then I could teach all day just like you did." I know the experience was extraordinary.

But saying such a thing sounds just like me in the prologue of this book. "Me, I got nothing." I have never had a conversation with someone who had the urge to write a book where within an hour, we could not pinpoint several powerful things that were worth writing about.

If you have the urge to write a book, do it.

The second point, using the story arc to create the presentation, is actually the most important. Talking for seven hours about an experience, however spectacular, would be boring and certainly not helpful to the audience.

Because I used the same process I teach in this book, I was able to consider carefully how to take the audience on a journey that would benefit them and leave them hopeful, empowered, and confident of their own capability.

This is my 12ᵗʰ book; I have at least three more books already on the drawing board.

I am confident that each one will be successful. I am confident that each will teach something important and useful to the right audience.

That confidence comes from knowing how to use the Story Arc™. I have given you this tool. It takes work, but it does work.

There is no need for you to say, as I did just a few years ago, "Me, I got nothing."

APPENDIX I

EDITING PROCESS

Every publisher has their own editing process. I will not attempt to give you the definitive approach to editing. This appendix is to share how I get a book ready for publication.

In chapter 37, I said, "Write, don't edit." If you follow that advice, when you get done with your dictation or with your typewritten manuscript, there will be many errors and things you don't think are your best and want to rewrite.

That is to be expected. When I am dictating, if I don't like how I said something or if I tell a story awkwardly, I don't stop to edit. I simply insert several returns, leaving a big space in the manuscript. In dictating software, this happens with verbal commands like speaking a message on your smartphone.

I do the same thing when I type. I just hit "enter" several times to create space. When I am finished, I go back to the manuscript and easily find those big spaces.

When I find them, I know this is a place I felt like something was not smooth or done well. Those are the first things I take a look at in editing. I get those fixed and then move into the editing process.

I break editing into three parts:

1. Writers edit.

2. Story or developmental edit.

3. Copy or line edit.

These different phases go by different names, so I'll explain what I mean so you can have a frame of reference if you talk to a publisher.

If you write a book all the way through as a first draft, you must do the first edit. I call this the "Writer's edit." Going all the way through the book, story arc in hand, making sure you have told the story you mean to tell, taught the things you meant to teach, and that it flows smoothly, is the writer's edit.

All the places you made mistakes and let them go as you wrote get fixed in this editing process. When this is complete, you should feel that the book is completed. It will take several passes through before you are satisfied you have said what you meant to say as well as you can.

Don't get stuck here. We're not aiming for perfection, just your best.

If despite your best efforts, you can't get it to a place you're ready for someone else to read it, you may need a ghostwriter to help with developmental work. Discuss this with your coach and your publisher (if you are not self-publishing).

The second edit should be done by someone else. There are several reasons for this. First, as the author, you know far too much detail about both the stories and the principles you are writing about.

Someone else must read this and see if they can follow clearly and easily through the threads you have woven. Some publishers send out copies to a few trusted readers and ask for markups. This is not a bad practice if you are content with the extra months may add to the production time of your book.

It will likely take at least a couple weeks to get mark-ups back. Then you need time to review and consolidate suggestions. It is an expanded version of using a single editor. The point is to have someone else read your book and make suggestions and edits.

How long this takes, how much it costs you, and the level of work depends on how much time you spend in the writer's edit.

Don't make the mistake of trying to "be the someone else" as you edit the book. Make the best edit you can in the first pass and then let a good editor do their job.

Some writers, especially newer authors, want an editor to use "track changes" as they do their editing. They are somehow terrified than an editor will "change their voice." This is unnecessarily limiting and makes it more difficult for a good editor to do their work.

If you feel you must supervise every change an editor makes, then either you need a different editor, or you need to accept the fact that professionals need to do their work.

Ultimately, as the author, you retain creative license and ownership, but making the editor unable to give you his or her best work by nitpicking every edit will slow down your creative process and ultimately be very frustrating.

After the second edit is complete, read it again and see if you think anything was missed or misunderstood. Since most word processors do track changes, you can turn it on and see what happened.

It will be difficult to follow if the editor moved things around or did some rewriting. That should not concern you. What should concern you is to see whether your stories remain faithful to your intent, and the principles you teach are clear and powerful.

The third editing process (whether it is called a line edit or a copy edit,) involves the laborious process of making sure every punctuation choice is correct, every verb tense is correct, word choices are accurate, passive versus active voice use is appropriate and all of the nitpicking grammar.

This may be done by the same person that does the second edit or by someone else. It must be someone familiar with good grammar editing tools and with the patience to read your book out loud, word for word, and see how it feels.

Many people claiming to be editors omit this "out loud" read. That is a fatal mistake. You cannot skim and pretend it is a thorough final edit. If you do, you will have typos and be embarrassed.

This is a flyover view of the three layers of editing.

If you want more detail on editing processes, tools, and resources, contact information is in appendix II.

Appendix II

Resources and Contact Information

I n my work as a coach, I am focused on helping people do things they don't believe they can do. That involves overcoming all the negative forces that convince us we are less than capable.

I have a lot of free resources available, including my new podcast: Your Ultimate Life Podcast with Kellan Fluckiger, on all of the popular podcast platforms.

Also, I upload new videos weekly on my YouTube Channel: Ultimate Life Formula. The URL is

https://www.youtube.com/c/UltimateLifeFormula.

Below is a list of all the resources referred to in this book and information about where to access them. All the books are available on Amazon, from the publisher or directly from me. They're listed below.

Also included is contact information if you want to contact the author, the publisher, or have further discussions about your book or inquire about coaching.

- *Walking Without Fear*
- *The Results Equation*
- *Meeting God at the Door*
- *The Tightrope of Depression*

- *The Book of Context*

- *Meditation, The Amazing Journey Within, Volume I*

- Volumes II-V of the Meditation series will be available soon.

- In addition, I conduct regular workshops on topics like:

- The Story Arc™

- Time Creation – Systems to Multiply Productivity

- Reading Magic – Systems to Read 10x faster than you read today

- Sales Systems – 4 Steps to Awesome Client Creation

- Creating Energy – Systems for Limitless Power

- Mastering Money – Understanding and Creating Wealth

- Learn to Meditate – guided meditation audio and video

I also conduct 90-day goal achievement workshops called *The Results Equation Intensive*. These are designed to help you accomplish a major goal in 90 days or less. They are held "virtually" and can be attended from anywhere.

I have other kinds of coaching arrangements to help people with any situation where they are finally committed to end addiction to mediocrity and create the life of their dream.

Contact information is below, and I welcome the opportunity to get to know you.

Email Kellan at: CoachKellanFluckiger@gmail.com

Website: www.kellanFluckiger.com

Contact the Publisher at: RedAussiePublishing@gmail.com

ABOUT THE AUTHOR

Kellan Fluckiger is the author of the #1 best-selling books *Tightrope of Depression, The Results Equation, The Book of Context, Meeting God at the Door, Meditation, The Amazing Journey Within,* and his latest book, *Walking Without Fear.*

He is an in-demand speaker and a highly successful coach. Working with CEOs of companies large and small, Kellan has touched and transformed many lives over the past 30 years.

A certified master coach and former C-suite Executive, Kellan has coached everyone from Super Bowl winners to BMI music award winners and everyone in between.

Kellan is a master at high achievement. As a motivational speaker and business coach, his journey has benefited thousands. He's written five books on meditation and provides coaching and support for creatives, entrepreneurs, and leaders on their journey through struggles and victories as they discover, develop, and manifest their talents to the world.

In addition to coaching, Kellan has written, recorded, and produced 11 albums of original music. He's been running a successful recording studio for over 35 years.

Samples of Kellan's music are available on his website at www.kellanfluckiger.com. You can also find his music on Amazon.

Born in San Francisco, CA, Kellan now spends most of the year creating and writing in Canada, with his wife, Joy, and their two cats and dogs.

Made in the USA
Columbia, SC
11 July 2020